Money Mastery Now!

4 Steps to Align with Money, Activate
Joy & Amplify Worth

Jenenne R. Macklin

Foreword By Les Brown

Contents

INTRODUCTION

Dedication

I dedicate this book to Ian Michael. You are and have been a precious gift that has blessed my life and heart with so much joy, laughter and growth, wrapped up in unconditional and unwavering love that cracked my heart open.

I am honored by your presence and hope I make you proud.

INTRODUCTION

Foreword

In this book, Jenenne tackles an uncomfortable subject. She talks about MONEY!!! Many of us don't like to talk about finances. But in *Money Mastery Now*, Jenenne takes you step by step from scarcity, to making a great salary but still facing major debts and not very good credit. Jenenne realized something had to change. And in that moment of clarity, she accepted what she had been doing was not working and made a decision to change. This birthed her *Align with Money* concept. Here, Jenenne recognized that money was a necessity and that scarcity was not the issue. She also understood that her mindset was the key. With the knowledge that there was enough for everyone, Jenenne made a choice to change consciously and unconsciously.

Jenenne did not get in her situation overnight. It took time to change and create a more prosperous future and present. This book is a must read for anyone wanting to change their financial situation for the better. It has strategic insights into our relationship with money. By applying the techniques in this book, readers can unconsciously begin to better their lives.

Money Mastery offers prosperity and mind set shifts that get you on the right track. These shifts help improve every aspect of life. By reading this book and applying these proven principles you can usher in prosperity and leave scarcity in the past.

Les Brown
February 22, 2019

Introduction

"If you want to change the fruits, you will first have to change the roots." – T. Harv Eker

What if I told you that you have the money thing all wrong? What if I told you that what you believe about money is a lie? What if the truth is you have everything you need to live a prosperous life?

For some, money is the driver that causes pain and worry. For others, money is a tool for success and fulfillment. And still for others, money literally cripples you and dismantles your sense of self-love and value. Your thoughts about money cause you to silently judge yourself because of the amount of money you do or do not have and because of what you think others think about you.

That's just the beginning.

But what if there was another way for you to think, speak and feel about money that could empower you and enhance your experiences?

This is what I offer you today. Begin with a clean slate recognizing that what you think about money might be completely off track. It is possible that the money stories you harbor and repeat, and the money worries you struggle with, are based on lies which rob you of happiness, peace of mind and success.

If you are struggling to build your savings, swimming in the deep end of credit card debt, longing for more fulfillment in your life or success in

your business, you have it
backwards. I know because I did.

You've been looking at that piece of
paper called money and thinking the
paper is all there is to it. You haven't
been given another possibility to
consider. Here is something new.
What if money is your birthright? In
other words, what if your spiritual
inheritance is waiting for you to
activate it through the awareness of
this truth? What if there really is
more than enough money and you've
been living from outdated money
beliefs that have been passed down
from generation to generation. What
if money really is your friend and is
waiting for you to unlock the
combination and receive the flow of
prosperity?

For many years, I believed what I
saw, heard and experienced when it
came to money. I don't remember

picking up a book or asking anyone questions about money's energy.

I basically did what my mother did and shared with me without question.

What has to happen for us to take the necessary actions to free ourselves from the grip of anxiety? What has to happen to stop us from feeling like we aren't enough or that we're out of time to create the life of our dreams? How can we live in a state of joy, fulfillment and happiness? If these are questions you've ever had, keep reading.

Today is the day you begin to unwrap and unpack what is influencing your money. You'll learn how you got it backwards and learn four powerful shifts to elevate your relationship with money.

We all have dreams, goals and desires that require money. That dream may consist of family vacations, home improvements, attending college, enjoying retirement and traveling the world. Your dream may be about building wealth and a family legacy or launching your own entrepreneurial or philanthropic endeavor. You long for the opportunity to live a quality life. Some of you have even attempted to map out what it would take to achieve your dream. You may question what keeps getting in the way of having the financial means to obtain it.

You work hard and make good money. This good money comes either from your own business or from your job, but you don't seem to be getting closer to living the life you've dreamed of. It always seems to be just out of your reach.

If this is your experience, I hope
you'll accept this invitation to move
from scarcity to prosperity. All that's
required is that you be totally honest.

Some of you reading this book
already know things you can do to
change your relationship with
money. When I was in that position,
I know I did. From reducing the
number of Starbucks stops I made in
a week, to intentionally decreasing
credit card usage. Eliminating
unplanned, unconscious and
unnecessary spending--you already
know where you can adjust. So, what
stops you from making changes?
You could have a savings fund,
experience less worry, gradually
build financial relief and experience
more peace of mind. Yet something
stops you each time you start. It's
time to seriously consider what has
prevented you from getting a handle

on the habits that rob you of peace of mind with money.

The Money Loop

For years, it seemed like I was in a money loop that felt like the spin cycle of a washing machine. Years later I started calling it the spin cycle. I felt like I was being tossed around. I constantly felt overwhelmed, fearful and worried about money. I had all these different schemes and possible solutions spinning around my mind as I tried to figure out how I was going to get out of the financial fix I was in...again.

I promised myself I'd save more or pay off a credit card or student loan. Little did I know those were simply lies that I told myself month after month because my actions said something different. It was also how I betrayed my sense of worth and value without even knowing it.

It was simple. Stop spending and start saving. For whatever reason that seemed like an uphill battle.

I told myself whatever I needed to, to let myself off the hook. I criticized myself for failing to follow through on my intentions. I felt trapped in the experience of my own unconscious creation.

Debt. Credit cards. Bill collectors. Bankruptcy. Zero to minimal savings. Not having any real money goals or plans for financial freedom kept me in the spin cycle. Fear and worry kept me panicked and anxious, which looked like me checking my bank account every morning worried that a check had bounced. If one had bounced, I worried about how I would cover it. If one hadn't bounced, I was good for the moment and released a sigh of relief. That only lasted until the next money moment.

I lived with the anxiety of what could happen that I wasn't prepared for. I was concerned about the next phone bill, credit card or car payment. I was living paycheck to paycheck. And even though this way of living was suffocating, in all honesty it wasn't enough to propel me to make a change. You know why? Because it was familiar. I knew my way around this crazy maze.

Maybe that was the missing link. I didn't know how to get myself out of the spin cycle or how to manage my financial future. I didn't know where to begin, and as my coach, Lisa Nichols says, "I didn't know what I didn't know." It would be years before I uncovered the truth.

What about you? Do you know what you need to know in order to plan your financial freedom and achieve your money/wealth goals?

What I know is that everything you desire is available to you now.

Infinite prosperity, wholeness, self-value, joy, love, happiness, peace, relief from worry and even financial freedom is available to you now. You can stop worrying and feeling frustrated with your money. You can start today by taking incremental steps that position you for more peace, self-confidence and relief with money.

I was seventeen years old and a senior in high school when I started a work study program. This means I began to handle money at a young age. Now I knew I should have saved money, but I didn't have the practice or the discipline to understand the significance of it. I didn't have the foresight to look ahead and plan. What I knew was that I was finally armed with what I could call *my money.* I contributed to the electricity and phone bill at my family home, so I rationalized that the rest of the money was mine to spend. I spent some on gas and clothes, put a little for savings and contributed my tithes.

Fast forward several years. I'm in my mid-thirties seeking to make my first home purchase. Sitting in the loan office with my bank specialist, I remember feeling unsure about the home buying process and the possibility of actually purchasing my first property. In spite of having gone to college and acquiring two degrees, I did not understand finances, nor did I fully understand the home buying process. I left the bank that day filled with sadness and shame.

No one knew I had a low credit score. No one knew how much money I had. What I did know was that my interest rate would be high because of my early money choices and spending habits.

My financial history was being tracked by the three spies. *Equifax, TransUnion* and *Experian*. Shame for not measuring up to some imaginary standard flooded my body as tears streamed down my face. At the same time, I was angry with myself and made a vow to wipe my tears, clean up my credit and get out of debt.

That was then. These days I am excited to live as a Professional Speaker, Wealth Catalyst and Mentor. I own two businesses. I speak and mentor men and women globally on how to change their relationship with money. While I empower people to know their value, live their value and charge for their value, I am passionate about eradicating scarcity and poverty thinking on the planet.

My most recent business emerged after being fired from my job in 2011. While being fired was somewhat of a surprise, my financial positioning was not. By then, I had a savings fund and an emergency fund. I took advantage of the 401(k)- retirement plan offered at my job because the company matched my contribution. I accrued a lot of vacation time because of a lack of self-care. When I was terminated, I received a totally separate check for my vacation time. My only debt was my home and my real estate. By then I had fallen in love with saving, which I'll share more about later. But aside from my real estate, I was debt free. My car was a 2001 Lexus that was in great condition. It was paid off, free and clear. I had no credit card debt.

How did a young Black girl who was orphaned at birth, later adopted and grew up in South Central Los Angeles on 108th between Main & San Pedro, get out of the money loop? How did I change my zip code and arrive at a life I love? A life rich with experiences of mentoring women throughout the world, traveling first-class (with the latest 2018 excursion being a trip to France with an amazing group of ladies to see Beyoncé & Jay Z in Nice). Later that year, I got to attend a Meet & Greet with Michelle Obama, the First Lady of the United States. I've had many high points on this journey. One was standing in front of nearly 2000 women and men in Atlanta, Georgia on the Speak & Write Conference stage with Lisa Nichols, world renowned coach. I was honored to share my expertise on ways to improve our relationship with money.

Another milestone was working with my first celebrity client and hopping a ride on a Gulfstream G6 Jet to travel to the Bahamas, which was the first of many of those trips.

This is in addition to the many audiences and stages I have been invited to speak on, as well as creating and hosting women's retreats at my home.

My greatest joy is in living the life I never thought would be possible–because I had not planned for it. Back then I couldn't see *how* to do it, but I knew I wanted to do something different. I didn't want to worry about money. Instead I wanted to learn how to manage my money responsibly. I no longer wanted to keep up with the Joneses. I wanted to be credit card debt free. My desire was to travel, spend time with my son as he was growing up, date and begin my philanthropic work. And that's just what I've done.

And you can too! Keep reading.

Why You? Why Now? Why Align?

Just as the above is true for me, let's empower your version of life to be true for you. It's important for you to understand that no one is coming to save you.

We rarely discuss our money or financial affairs with others fearing judgment for our poor decisions. We may even be embarrassed by our financial predicament. Secondly, our relationship with money is something that is personal since we are the CEO of our financial affairs. From my point of view, it is imperative that we take control and accept responsibility for our financial decisions and ultimately our financial independence. Here are a few reasons why.

Why You?
Why you? Because you wield more power than you know.

You are not using it. You are a Queen or Kin who is unsure of his or her power and is using it willy-nilly and driving yourself crazy.

Why you? Because you are the power center of your success. Instead of grabbing it by the reigns, you are hiding and peeking out, waiting for someone or something to change things to make it easier for you. It's important to me that you understand, in this and every moment, that you are the YOU that you've been waiting for. It's not him or her that will rescue you – only you.

Why you? Because these are the hard-core facts: Women are paid less than men for the same work. Women are usually left alone to manage our financial lives after a divorce or the death of a spouse. Women tend to discredit their ability to learn and understand concepts of finances.

We shy away from investing in matching programs at our jobs or in the stock market because of afraid of losing money. This is a common reason why women tend to keep their money in checking and savings accounts where they lose instead of gain interest.

Why you? Because the conscious or unconscious decision to remain financially illiterate is unacceptable and something we can no longer afford to do given that at some point on our journey we will have to manage our finances.

Why you? Because you matter to me, to yourself and to this world. We are better contributors when we are free of money worries and have control over our money rather than having it control us. *Why you?* Because our tendency to hide our money issues and not seek help or engage in conversations with others about money, encourages unconscious spending habits that rob us of our joy.

Why now?
The world is changing, and we must be prepared. Research shows that women control over $20 trillion in

worldwide spending. In the U.S., women control more than 60% of all personal wealth. Women account for 85% of all consumer purchases. 75% of women are identified as the primary shopper for their households. From electronics, travel, automobiles, sports (yes, the NFL, NBA, NHL and MLB female fans), technology, healthcare, food, business, careers and education, women are all in.

60% of millennials ages 18-29 are single and 20% are moms. Many Gen-X women feel they are in a financial position that is worse than they expected.

80% of today's women are *Empty Nesters*. Boomer women or women ages 50+, make up every fifth adult in the United States. Baby Boomers are actually the healthiest, wealthiest and most active generation in women's history controlling a net worth of $19 trillion. You can count me in this group.

*Source Demographics by Mark Miller.

Boomers are considered marquee players in the game of finance. They are educated, have high incomes and make 95% of the purchasing decisions in their home (Karen Vogel, The Women's Congress: She-economy).

What this says is women have money.   The deeper question is what are we doing with the money we have? Since we have money, why are we so closed mouth about claiming our financial freedom?

Do you realize that when it comes to talking about money, being knowledgeable and strategic...mum's

the word? Think about it, we will
talk all day with our girlfriends about
our personal affairs. We'll talk about
marriage, relationships and dating
and even some medical issues. But
when it comes to talking about
money and wealth, we get tight
lipped.

The world around us is changing and
that change is a sign that we need to
be prepared. According to *Single
Women and Money*, a new piece of
research from Fidelity Investments,
single women are deeply concerned
about their finances. The question is,
are we concerned enough to take
action?

Some of us think someone is going to
rescue us from the stress we feel
about money. The truth is, the time
has come for us to rescue ourselves.

For millennials who want to get married or become mothers, know that neither being married or being a parent exempts us from the need to plan our financial future. When you think someone is going to rescue you, there's a tendency not to take strategic action. But taking action can save your life and ensure you have the resources to survive major challenges.

Unfortunately, many of us make our mark on the world through our spending habits and related addictions. There is market analysis and research geared toward our directing our spending.

The marketing industry counts on women in particular. Their impulse buying, tendency to spend recklessly and chase sales. Sale tactics are designed to attract gender specific spending habits. All the shiny objects at check-out registers in just about every store is designed with women in mind. I began to notice women how get taken by marketing techniques in stores that are created to draw them in. Once I understood what was happening, I realized we have a choice to stick to our budget, savings plan or financial goals. And if women aren't the target, the next target is our children who looks at the shiny objects and repeatedly ask, "Can I get this?"

I realized that 1) We live in a capitalist country so I can't get mad at the game and, 2) As women we have the full right and authority to say no to anything that takes us off our plan.

The question is why more of us don't say no or ignore the shiny objects. As one woman in my Real Money

Matters online group once said, "I buy what I don't need and don't use."

Herein lies the insight to our spending habits and addictions. Feeling a sense of worth and value often drives our spending rather than our desired goals and fulfillment.

So *Why Now*? Because at the rate your emotions are spending your money, you will never be able to live the life you desire. Nor will you have the relationship with money that'll sustain you in building wealth or a solid legacy.

Why Align?
If your journey with money has been anything like mine, then just like me, you have it backwards when it comes to money. What I mean is, there is a spiritual and invisible aspect to money that no one told us about.

This is the secret that millionaires know and live according to. Money is about more than a piece of paper with nice pictures.

Money is more than your thoughts and thinking. Money is all about emotions...your heart. Therefore, money itself is an emotional vibration and feeling which brings me to a popular topic for some of you – The Law of Attraction (LOA).

At its core, LOA is really the law of your vibration and energy, and we will get to that later. Your vibration is the invisible aspect of money that you're missing. I was in my mid-forties before I began to connect the invisible dots about money, mindset, wealth and financial freedom. This was not only revealed to me in my reading and research but also in my conversations and coaching with women outside of the United States.

Do you know that there are women who have never held a negative thought about money? Do you know that there are women who were only taught that money was a tool to be used?

Nothing about not having enough money. Nothing about the rich getting rich while the poor get poorer. This made me wonder, what is the difference between women in the U.S. and elsewhere? Why do so many women I mentor in the United States live with thoughts of scarcity and limitations around money, while women I coach who live outside the United States operate more from the thought that prosperity is their birthright? Could it simply be a matter of the information we are taught about money?

Pause and ask yourself, where did I get my money thoughts, habits and ideas? If your answer is like so many that I've heard over the years, you would say you got them from your family of origin, your parents and your culture. This explains the need for realignment.

Align the way you think, speak and feel about money to embrace the truth that money is the outward expression of an invisible vibration.

The power to align is innate. The definition of being in alignment with money is, "to bring into alignment your thoughts, words, feelings and actions with the energy of money." This means, you don't have to look anywhere but inside of yourself. You have the power within to align your relationship with money for greater results in your life.

I took incremental steps toward changing the way I handled money. I had to talk about it. I had to think about it and plan. It's interesting how the same tool or instrument that caused my frustration, fear and worry about money could be used to create the life I desired. The success we seek, the happiness and fulfillment we long for--all is connected to our relationship with money.

We must recognize that aligning our relationship with money is a day-to-day process. We have to start where we are. For example, how would you describe your current relationship with money? Next identify the actions and thoughts that contributed to where you are in relation to money. Then look forward to where you want to be and plot a course of action to achieve your goals.

Here's what I know, if I can do it, so can you – if you're determined to do so. You can learn how to get out of the spin cycle in your financial affairs and begin to experience greater confidence with money.

This is my personal invitation for you to get out of the Money Loop, align your relationship with money and plan your financial path to prosperous living and thinking, NOW!

Chapter One-The Missing Link

"Change your thoughts, change your life."
Dr. Wayne W. Dyer

My life journey has been a call to dive deeper into understanding money, its myths, mysteries and especially what I call the invisible aspects of money. There had to be more to money than the experience I was having. How could one person make a certain amount of money and have one experience, while another person making the same amount of money has a completely different experience? Since money itself is a neutral energy I tried to find out what was the determining factor between those two experiences.

I view money as a neutral energy because it can't and doesn't create itself. Money is simply a piece of paper with nice pictures of men on it. But what does it represent?

More importantly, what do we need to understand to make better choices with our money and change our relationship with the power of money?

Money is an Inside Job

I thought having money was simply a matter of earning it and knowing what to do with it after I got it. It would be years before I would understand that everything was connected, which included me and the money I made. Money and I weren't as separate as I thought. Instead, money was connected to the same source I was connected to.

What connected me and money was my mindset. On another level, it was the invisible aspects of life that connected me and money. What does that mean? At the core, money and I are made out of the same substance – energy. Energy is physics and energy, as Albert Einstein taught us, is in everything and everything has energy.

Energy is drawn from the invisible aspects of life. It manifests as our dreams, books, products, etc. Look around where you are at this moment. As you do, remember that everything you see, where you are in this moment, was once invisible. Where you are was once an idea inside of someone's mind that was cultivated to manifest. Everything starts inside and then goes through the process of manifesting as a reality. The same is true for you. Given the fact that money is energy, there is never a scarcity of money or the opportunity to align our energy with money.

It wasn't until in my mid 30's, after my mother made her transition (also known as having passed away) that I began to pull back the curtain to gain greater insights on what I refer to as the invisible, non-physical aspects of life. I had completed spiritual training in the *New Thought Metaphysical* teachings. Having grown up attending the *Tabernacle of Faith Baptist Church* in Los Angeles, where I extensively read and studied the Bible, the metaphysical religious training gave me a deeper understanding of the sacred text beyond a literalist view. Later, as an adult, I attended the *Church of Inner Light* led by Rev. Trudy Garno. It was after that I felt drawn to ministerial training. I delayed that training because of my mother's fight with cancer.

Intuition would later lead me to enroll in a two-and-a-half-year metaphysical training and be ordained as a minister. It was through this training that I learned about the invisible energetic aspect of life. Many were aware of this aspect through few talked about or addressed it. And that invisible aspect includes all things that are visible on the planet including me, you, and of course, money.

Living from this spiritual perspective helped me view life a different way-- through the lens of possibility, potential, power and presence. This is a perspective that unites all of us as whole spiritual beings who are interconnected. We have been brought into physical expression i.e. human form, by One Power, that is omnipresent, omnipotent, and omniscient.

Throughout this book you'll hear me reference God, Life and the Universe as a way of capturing this infinite perspective. I do this in recognition of the vastness of God. Using one word to describe the God energy is too small and may fall short of describing the magnitude of God.

As I continued to study, I recognized one of the biggest misconceptions about money--one that impacts some, cripples' others and robs all who agree with it--is the lie that there is scarcity in the world. Many of us were fed the story of scarcity and the belief that there is limitation. When we are taught that there is not enough love, food, money, promotions or even compliments for everyone, we also believe that when someone else receives we lose. This is untrue. The truth is, when someone else wins it increases our chances of getting what we desire.

I have no doubt that these beliefs are real to many people. They certainly felt real to me every day when I lived them. What I know now is that we live, move and have our Being in a prosperous Universe. Just as there is no scarcity of air, gravity, blades of grass, leaves on the trees, sunsets or grains of sand on the beach, there is no scarcity of prosperous living, money, wealth and happiness. There are sufficient opportunities, resources, ideas, innovation, love, joy and fulfillment for everyone.

If it's true that there is no lack, then what causes the gap between what many of us have lived for so many years and the minute-by-minute truth demonstrated by the Universe? Look no further than inside yourself.

It is our thinking that makes scarcity real in your lives. This way of thinking and living unconsciously keeps us stuck when it comes to money.

The answer can be found in Dr. Dyer's quote at the beginning of this chapter, "Change your thinking, change your life."

This quote is connected to another quote in Money Mastery Now which says, "When you want to change the fruit, you must first change the roots." In this analogy the roots represent what is within us, such as our beliefs, consciousness, mindset and thinking – the invisible aspects of us. The fruits are our dreams, goals, plan, vision and results. When we change from the inside, we align with our dreams and goals. That's when the outer results we desire show up.

The inside job is to cultivate the belief that there is more than enough money. The inside job is to align with the power you have to create more and live a prosperous life. The inside job is to send a vibrational frequency to the Universe at the highest vibration that you can.

Everything begins within. The same way a seed is planted in dark rich soil, unseen and hidden from sight. Over time, it pushes through to the sun to sprout. This process represents how to plant seeds of thoughts in our consciousness and push them through until they show up in our lives.

Prosperity Is Yours

Everything you want is available to you now. Absolute prosperity, joy, happiness, wealth, fulfillment, success and financial freedom.

Unbeknownst to you, you are surrounded by prosperity at all times, especially when you understand that prosperity includes the quality of your thinking and living. When many people hear the word prosperity their first thought is success and financial well-being. This is just the tip of the iceberg.

Prosperity speaks to the wholeness and quality of your life. It suggests the promise of a happy, fulfilled, living experience on this planet. Living in prosperity can be a tangible, day-to-day reality when you understand the missing links in your relationship with money.

What Is Prosperity?
Here is the definition of prosperity I have lived by since first reading about it over 30 years ago. It came from a book by Eric Butterworth titled *Spiritual Economics: The*

Principles and Process of True Prosperity. I've read this book many times.

Butterworth writes, "Prosperity is a way of **living** and **thinking** and not just money. Poverty is a way of **living** and **thinking** and not just a lack of money or things."

There you have it. To be prosperous is to cultivate a particular way of thinking about life and the circumstances that impacts the quality of your living.

This is significant because so many people define prosperity by the amount of money or financial success they've experienced. They forget prosperity includes the ease in which we attain success in our ventures, thriving in our endeavors and feeling accomplished in simply living our life.

43

When you look at it in the broadest sense, prosperity speaks to our overall spiritual well-being. Being happy in our day-to-day living, experiencing peace, good health, confidence and inner fulfillment.

It's not just about the money because you and I both know people with money who still struggle in their relationships, health, family issues and day-to-day living. In spite of having thousands or even millions of dollars they are still unhappy. I know what you're thinking. You're thinking you'd rather have the millions and be unhappy than not have them. Really? Think about that. I can say from experience that I've had thousands of dollars in the bank and having money did not change the problems I had. Imagine that.

The biggest mistake you can make is to define yourself by your circumstances or what has happened to you. In reality your inner thinking (mindset) and consciousness have far more to do with your quality of living.

The only way to live on a prosperous planet and experience lack with our fundamental needs is by not having the financial knowledge i.e. the missing links.

We also need disciplined living and thinking to manage the money we do have. Bottom line, prosperity is a birthright. It's your innate divine inheritance.

It's Your Mindset

According to Stanford psychologist Dr. Carol Dweck, your beliefs play a pivotal role in what you want, what you think you can achieve and whether or not you will achieve it. Dr. Dweck believed it is your mindset that determines your achievements and successes.

There are two kinds of mindsets that we operate from: fixed and growth. The fixed mindset believes what you see is what you get. The growth mindset believes the sky is the limit...if I can see it, I can achieve it.

Your mindset will determine how you relate to money, how you see your access to prosperity and your ability to achieve your financial freedom. It also lends to your level of happiness, fulfillment, wealth creation and legacy building.

This is why you will hear me, and other experts say that it doesn't matter if you change banks, pay off your credit cards or promise to be smarter about your money. If you aren't aware of your mindset, you might be struggling against yourself because of being hardwired by your beliefs.

Pause for a moment to reflect. Ask yourself if you believe in your stated goals? Do you believe you're worthy of peace of mind, financial relief, family vacations, consistent savings, comfortable retirement, college funds, real estate and investment capital? Notice how you feel as you think about achieving these goals.

Are you excited and eager to take up the task or hesitant and overwhelmed to the point of being immobilized? The answer to these questions can be found in your growth or fixed mindset.

Why Your Mindset Matters

Your mindset is a critical factor in how you respond to life's challenges whether it is deciding to look for a job, attend college or pass a college exam. When you operate from a fixed mindset there is a need for approval before stepping out because you are afraid you might fail. Most decisions are made based on thoughts of success or failure and whether you will look dumb or smart when it's all said and done. When you have a growth mindset you persevere, hang in there and do whatever it takes because you are determined to reach your goals.

The growth mindset has a hunger for learning, exploring and accepting life's challenges. There's also a willingness to tackle problems head on. The growth mindset knows that in the process you will grow as a person.

Where Did Your Mindset Come From?
According to Dr. Dweck, our mindset training starts during childhood. We can see how that training shaped our lives by answering the following questions.

1. Were you more focused on looking smart or "being" smart and loving learning?

2. Were you willing to explore and embrace new experiences?

3. Did and do you view setbacks as part of life on the road to achieving your goal or do you shy away after a setback?

Now, think for a minute about your beliefs about money and your current relationship with money.

4. What is your mindset about achieving financial freedom? Are you excited to follow through and take action? Or are you overwhelmed by the thought of it all?

Here are some statements about mindsets that may give you a better understanding of the teaching in this chapter. You can explore these statements further by taking the Mindset Test which is found in the Resource Section of this book.

Which of these do you agree with?

- No matter who you are there isn't much you can do to improve your basic abilities and personality. True or False
- You can learn new things and improve your intelligence. True or False
- People either have talent or they don't. True or False

The key here is to know yourself and your abilities. Knowing yourself allows you to recognize how your mindset effects your choices when you encounter challenges in life and with money.

My Mindset Evolving

When I was growing up on the east side of Los Angeles, in the hood, I wasn't clear about what I wanted. I learned what I wanted by watching and following others.

I attended Locke High School, a school that was built because there wasn't a school for the neighborhood students. Busing us to the west side for school wasn't an option. My working-class parents gave me one primary responsibility and that was to attend school. I was a B/C student and didn't get much help with homework. I didn't even think about going to college. No one in my family discussed college nor were there role models for me to turn to.

Two people who impacted my decision about going to college were my school counselor, Marguerite Archie and my classmate Ronald White. Mrs. Archie would *tell* our class we were going to college. She proceeded to help us with testing and filling out college applications. My classmate Ronald was significant because we grew up together, attend the same church, junior high and high schools.

Ronald was smart, hands down. I, on the other hand, was not. But since we were from the same community and church, I told myself that if he could do it, so could I. He had no clue I was using him as my motivation.

I don't remember my exact scores, but I didn't score very high on the Standardized Achievement Test (SAT). Still I applied to colleges as directed by Mrs. Archie and was accepted into Whittier College in Los Angeles. I was also placed on the waiting list for University of Southern California.

I accepted the invitation from Whittier College because admission was guaranteed. If I had been aware of the elite status that going to USC meant, I would have waited and gone there. As a young Black girl without understanding of the role college can play in one's professional development, I jumped at the first sure opportunity. Ronald was accepted to Loyola Marymount University, which is also in Los Angeles. We stayed in close contact.

I didn't fare well in college since I was unprepared. I didn't have good study skills. I didn't fully comprehend the work, especially statistics. I wasn't very good at test-taking and barely passed some of my freshman year classes. I was dating a Senior named Bruce Talamon who suggested I enroll in a student exchange program to Denmark. He said, "When you come back, you'll know if you want to continue in college or quit."

I did exactly what Bruce said. I enrolled in the student exchange program. I worked the Summer before the Fall semester so I would have money for my trip. Since my father worked for United Airlines, my travel to and from the Netherlands was secure. This is when I learned how knowing and talking to the right people can make a difference in your life.

Going on the student exchange program to a country I had never even heard of and didn't do any research on was transformational. I traveled with a HUGE Winnie the Pooh teddy bear, a box of Cheerios and the book, *The Autobiography of Malcom X*.

My school performance in the Netherlands wasn't that much better than in the U.S., but I passed. While the program was conducive to studying, it was even more conducive to travelling. Our school week was only four days which left the full weekend for travel. My classmates and I would often hop on a train and travel the countryside. I took solo trips to by boat to Norway and Sweden.

By saying yes to the exchange program, I gained a different perspective of myself as a Black woman who was admired and accepted rather than ridiculed. I developed confidence in myself and in my ability to navigate the unknown. I also learned how to take care of myself and figured out how to get help when I needed it. I learn about other cultures, languages and customs. I learned that the world was enormous. That expanded my mindset on so many levels.

Just as my friend Ronald predicted, I returned to school in the U.S. with a new attitude. My last two years of college were great! I was able to refine my focus even more when another student on campus told me, "It seems like you'd be better in social work than in business."

Girl was she right!!! I excelled in the Sociology track and graduated as a B student.

From there I applied to graduate school and earned my master's degree in Social Work, graduating as an A student. I've often marveled at how
I attended graduate school after struggling so much as an undergraduate student. While I was doing the school thing, I continued to keep in touch with Ronald, my junior high/high school friend. When I went to graduate school at California State University in Sacramento, he attended Hastings Law School in San Francisco. Even though we primarily partied together rather than discussed or studied school, it meant a lot to me that someone close to me was on the same academic journey.

After completing graduate school, I started my first company, Adolescent Management Systems, Inc. to provide mental health services to my favorite population, adolescent boys. All that I did was all driven by my evolving mindset and perspective about my skills, abilities and potential for success.

Let's be clear, I'm not suggesting you go to Europe. However, if you're in college for the first time and you've never traveled internationally, then yes, I am. It's not the trip as much as it is about what you'll learn from the trip. It's also about how the resources and information you connect with while traveling can help move you forward.

Your circumstances don't have to define you or your life. What matters most is what you think and are open to experiencing. I say this because I know the stories of people like my beloved mentor and coach, Lisa Nichols, who is the most requested motivational speaker in the country and the best-selling author of six books. The story of Les Brown, mega motivational speaker, author, disc jockey and politician.

I can't forget one of my favorite metaphysical teachers, Joe Vitale, whose work is synonymous with the Law of Attraction and who started his journey living on the streets. Each had humble beginnings and challenging circumstances. From Lisa living in a neighborhood impacted by gang violence to Les and his brother being adopted by a woman who had love, discipline and guidance to offer – they all made the decision to excel despite the odds.

I'm pretty sure they didn't have a conscious awareness about their mindset in the old days. What they knew was, they *had* to change their lives because no one was going to do it for them. And, if they could do it, if I can do it. And so, can you.

Mindset and My Credit Cards

The reason mindset became so important to me was because of my experience with credit card debt. As soon as I accepted the first invitation to get a credit card I was in debt. I ended up struggling with debt not once but twice. That's right. I had to learn the lesson *twice.*

I made a decision to move to financial freedom both tangibly and emotionally. I did the research and hired a consolidation company to pay off all my debt. After six months of making consistent payments, I was excited about the possibility of being debt free. With each payment my frustration eased, my shame lessened, and my disappointment gave way to self-confidence. After 16 months, I was free! I enjoyed the feeling of relief which felt like a breath of fresh air. A burden and weight had been lifted from my heart.

About one year later I started talking to myself. I convinced myself I could use my credit cards again and how this time, I would manage them better. But I wasn't doing anything differently. I hadn't changed my habits, nor had I tied my financial goals and success to a plan. What I told myself was, now that I understood how to manage credit I would do better. I didn't like the feeling of being in debt or being riddled with fear and anxiety over bills.

You'd think that going through the process of paying off my credit cards would've been enough to stop me from getting in debt a second time. But paying off my credit cards was simply a left-brain function. What was missing was the right-brain connection and the ability to reset my thinking and feelings.

I learned that both a head and heart connection was necessary for financial wellness. Without both, I was destined to repeat my actions.

What I Heard Growing Up

I soon understood that the way I handled money was based on conversations I'd overheard from my mom and family. Growing up I heard the occasional yelling and arguing between my parents over my father's gambling and the financial and emotional toll his spending had on the family. I also heard comments from our friends and neighbors about how proper I talked and how nice my clothes were. They thought I came from a rich family and I thought I had to play that role. What they didn't know was that my mother was a heck of a seamstress.

My mother always had her *Singer* sewing machine set up in our dining room ready to use. The fact that many of my dress clothes were sewn by my mother didn't get me off the hook.

I also remember getting conflicting messages about money. People from my church and my community saw us in Beverly Hills. I went with my mother, who at the time was a private duty nurse to several celebrities. These imprints and influences on my relationship with money would later unravel.

What Is Your Measure

I recently interviewed a woman who I was considering becoming a private coaching client. She had purchased a home, had a full-time job, made a mid-range six-figure salary.

She had minimal savings and was fairly satisfied with where she was professionally. She did not know how to move to the next level. She did not know what to focus on for wealth building nor was she aware of how her mindset contributed to defining her goals of financial freedom. Having a six-month emergency savings fund, maxing out her 401(k) contribution and investing were not in her forecast. It was clear that her desire for greater wealth was being thwarted by inaccurate messages. Messages that had been passed down by her parents rather than created by her own personal capacity. She was being called to make a change. I was prepared to support her 100%.

You Already Have What You Seek

Like me, many of us hit the ground running when we get our first job. Without any skills, knowledge or understanding about money, we gobble up the invitation to become members of the credit card carrying community. We think it will give us more spending power and maybe even the personal status of having arrived.

However, not having knowledge about money or wealth wisdom we don't understand the mindset, discipline and planning needed to avoid being on a fast track to debt and heartache.

While you may worry, fret, fuss and complain like I did for years, in the end, your future is in your hands. You have what you are seeking. You've just been looking for it in the wrong place.

You have the power to control what you do or don't do with your money. You have the power to determine what you believe, save, spend, share, invest or splurge on shiny objects.

You possess the power necessary to move towards relief, ease and peace of mind with money. So, what's stopping you?

What Does a Good Relationship with Money Feel Like?

After four plus years of living with Multiple Myeloma, a form of blood cancer, my mother made her transition. She had followed the doctor's orders to rest more, eat cleaner and exercise in the hope of regaining full health at the five-year mark. But in the end, she made her journey home to be with God.

When she transitioned, I inherited our family home and what I considered then to be a large sum of money. For the first time in my life, I had money that I could actually spend that wasn't already spent and accounted for before it came in. I had always wondered what it felt like to buy something and not have to worry about the cost. To not feel remorseful, worried or anything other than gratitude after spending money.

I still remember that day. I drove fifteen miles to go shopping at the mall. I perused the big-name department stores for something that caught my eye. I settled on an expensive designer handbag. I paid cash for it. It was exhilarating to buy what I wanted!! It felt as if I had tapped into a secret vault of feelings and emotions. I felt expansive, like something bigger than the purchase was awakened within me. This is the feeling that comes from being able to spend money guilt-free.

That's the feeling I want for every single one of you reading this book. To experience relief, joy and confidence in your money relationship and to live from that perspective.

To understand and live in that space, not just for a moment but for the rest of your life.

Energetic Sidekicks for Success: Courage, Commitment, Consistency

At the end of a previous chapter I asked readers, "If you already have what you're seeking then what's stopping you?"

What was your answer?

If you don't know, I want to tell you what is stopping you is Y-O-U.

Sometimes we have to be sick and tired of being sick and tired. We have to be tired of stressing and struggling to make ends meet. You have to tell yourself you want something different and follow that want by taking action.

With each sale that flashes on the television screen--for every high-end store coupon you receive or pop-up shop that comes to town, you have to remind yourself of your goals. That takes Courage, Commitment and Consistency.

COURAGE
It takes courage to be responsible for your financial life, especially since many of us weren't groomed for this position. This is something no one can do for us. We must tap into an infinite reservoir of courage to become financially responsible for our life and future. This means being strategic, confident, knowledgeable and enlightened about money and wealth from its visible and invisible aspects.

It means taking a stand for your financial freedom at all costs. *What will it cost me?* you ask. It will cost you no longer repeating the same unconscious habits or ignoring them as if they don't exist.

No longer can you ignore the power of a budget to tell your money where to go before your feelings do. No longer can you think that a man, a marriage, a buy-out, a pay-out, an inheritance or sugar daddy will be your financial freedom rescuer. No longer can you lie to yourself by saying, "When I get...I will..." No longer can you deny the innate power and inherent God-given gifts you have been endowed with to create wealth in your life. No longer can you guess about the monthly revenue in your business. No longer can you chase money like you chase a sale or a man. No longer can you place the needs and demands of others ahead of your goal of financial success.

A famous quote by Eleanor Roosevelt says, "You must do the things you think you cannot do." If you are reading this, I have no doubt that this isn't the first time you've looked at your relationship with money and realized that something has GOT to change.

Pause right here. Put the book down for a moment and ask yourself:

What stops me from taking a different action with money?

What is telling me I can't do this?

Listen for the answer and write it in your journal.

Whatever your answer, it is only one of the reasons you must activate your courage and stand face-to-face with your internal doubts. The way you've been juggling and stressing about money has been hard.

This is an invitation for you to take those struggles and shift them in another direction – the direction of financial freedom.

Merriam Webster defines courage, as "mental or moral strength to venture, persevere and withstand danger, fear or difficulty." This is a call for you to tap into your fearlessness. It's an invitation to know yourself at your core and claim the prosperity that has been waiting for you. It is an invitation to tap into the BOLD idea of a greater purpose for your life. You want something different for your money. It's time to create a plan, step out and do something about it.

The byproduct of standing in courage is that you won't stand alone – trust me I know. What will rise up in you is the power and strength to persevere. You will strengthen your determination and awaken something greater within.

Courage moves you to remember the truth of who you are and the innate power that resides within you. Rather than thinking of this as a problem to be solved, consider it an opportunity to expand, evolve and elevate. With each act of courage, you are calling forth the prosperity that dwells within.

Remember as you continue to take action your fear will gradually dissipate. The stories you told yourself about what would happen if you took action didn't happen.

How did you feel after taking action? Were you excited or nervous? Were you aware of a deeper power within supporting you through the process?

Courage may be a new muscle for you to exercise and you may be a little sore at first. Trust me it won't last long.

The more willing you are to be courageous the closer you will get to the truth of who you are.

It takes courage to think thoughts that are aligned for greater results. It takes courage to say no. Your past actions gave people the message that you would be the fixer for their financial mistakes or poor money management habits. It takes courage to say no more.

It will take courage to look at your budget each week and adjust it as needed. It will take courage to say no to yourself when you want to soothe yourself with a purchase that provides momentary relief. It will take courage to stand for your results until they become visible and evident.

COMMITMENT

There is a saying, "How you do one thing, is how you do all things."

How do we make and keep commitments? More specifically, how do you keep your commitments to yourself?

Women, in particular, are very familiar with making commitments to others. Whether it's your boss or staff, school committees, your church or the PTA. Most of us easily hand out commitment chips to others. But to give our courage legs strength, we must make a total and complete commitment to ourselves and our financial success. This commitment speaks directly to how much we value ourselves, our energy, time and money.

Where do you stand with being financially responsible for yourself and your life? What does it mean to have greater confidence, knowledge and tools in your relationship with money? I didn't think of commitment unless it involved someone I was dating or in a relationship with.

Our commitment to financial wellness is no different than making a commitment to release ten pounds of excess weight. Commitment to changing your relationship with money is no different than a commitment to complete a graduate degree, run a marathon, create a musical piece, start a family or build a business. The commitment came from within you.

If you tapped into it once you can tap into it again. For it to work you must do what author Steven Covey says, "Start with the end in mind."

When your commitment wavers, ask yourself what was the motivation for you to make that commitment? Were you motivated from within?

When we make commitments because of an external pressure or because of a need to be accepted, the commitment typically won't last for the duration of the journey. Why? Well, nothing outside of you has greater power than what is inside of you. Therefore, all of your commitments must be ignited from within your spirit and heart.

Let's start with this. What's your vision for becoming financially fit? Will you track your spending each week on a budget? Will you put aside X amount of money in a savings fund? Will you become debt free or decrease your debt by fifty percent? These are commitments that will transform your relationship with money.

Each of these ideas require action to complete. When I went through this process, I made a commitment to becoming financially fit.

I made a commitment to my health after discovering I was gluten intolerant. I made a commitment to stop driving fast and instead leave earlier for appointments.

I also made a commitment to meditate each morning, to be more conscious of my thoughts and words.

You are making a pledge to understand money, to have more peace with money and to taking the actions that will change your relationship with money. You are making a declaration to yourself and the Universe to honor the money you already have by monitoring how you spend, save and share your money. You are committing to place yourself first in your thinking, speaking and actions in order to achieve your goals.

Once we make a commitment, we must take action.

We put one foot in front of the other until courage turns to fuel and propels our dreams forward.

You are not doing this alone anymore. You have declared to the Universe that you welcome divine wisdom, guidance, resources and strategies to live in an aligned relationship with prosperity. We're not just talking about money. This is about getting into alignment for prosperous living and thinking.

At the core of your being, there is an aspect of you that knows you are here to live a prosperous life and is eager to assist you on the journey. You just have to keep moving forward and being persistent even when things are hard.

CONSISTENCY

Whether you know it or not we all have some level of flow, routine or schedule that we use to maneuver through life.

I have friends who follow a consistent routine that they live by every day, while others are consistent with flexibility. Flexibility varies from day-to-day, but it is anchored in an overall routine. The key here is taking regular, steady inspired action until your desire or dream is manifested.

Consistency is the secret sauce of producing a desired result. Merriam

Webster defines the word consistent as "marked by harmony, regularity or steady continuity." Also, consistency is defined as the "condition of adhering to, persistency, harmony of conduct or practice." You are being called to be in harmony with your goals by taking steady, persistent, inspired action.

I find that it's not so much the goal but our moment to moment action toward fulfilling that goal. As we get closer to reaching our goal, we become more excited and anxious. Some subconsciously sabotage their own efforts by making excuses or justifications why we didn't keep our daily commitment. When this happens, pay attention to internal conversations and underlying feelings.

What is the overarching feeling that robs you of your freedom? Most will find the villain to be nothing other than the usual suspect–fear. When you step up to face and achieve your goals, of course, fear pops up. You don't have to give in to it. You can honor your feelings and continue to place one foot in front of the other. Know that with each action you take, you are standing up for your goals. You are getting closer to the results you long for.

Courage. Commitment. Consistency. These three energetic sidekicks will give you a greater sense of confidence and ignite you with a sense of worth from within. Only then, can you operate from a place of true prosperity.

Take control of your financial decisions and create your desired

results with the missing links for
financial freedom.

Chapter Two-Align Your

Thoughts:

Money Myths
"You have the power to think deliberate thoughts that will show up as your reality." Jenenne Macklin

Your Thoughts are Things

"Our thoughts are things," is a powerful statement to embrace and live as an aspect of our self-perception. We can also shift that quote to say, "My thoughts are the things that show up in my life." This positions us to step into our full power to create the life we want.

Until I was able to make this crucial connection, I felt like a victim most of my life. Someone or something was always doing something to me.

As I embraced the idea that my thoughts have the power to attract and create the experiences in my life, I found relief to a degree. On one hand, I was no longer at the will of others but on the other hand, I was now more responsible for my life than before. I realized that I am and have been responsible for *all* the things that happened in my life.

Here's what I put together through my reading, studying and testing.

Science has determined that the entire universe consists of two elements: matter and energy. Through this combination, everything has been created–including you.

We transmit energy into the Universe with our thoughts. When energy is transmitted through our thoughts, it returns to us as the source and creator of them. When we accept this as our reality, we tap into the intangible laws of the universe, such as the law of gravity. We use these universal laws to attract what we desire into our lives.

Here's another example of this principle. Once upon a time you were just a microcosm of a tiny, invisible cell. That cell became a divine spark of creativity, a thought in Divine Mind brought forth into physical expression.

This confirms the fact that our thoughts are powerful things. They carry a vibration that broadcasts to the universe. This signal is matched with other complementary signals until it shows up in a physical form.

87

When you know what you desire and allow it to become a dominant thought in your awareness, you become, as the English poet W.E. Hentley wrote, "The master of your fate; the captain of your soul." In other words, you have the power to *cultivate and control your thoughts*.

It may be hard to believe that you can control your thoughts. You have so many of them. What I'm saying is that you can train your thoughts to attract what you want in your life. Just like when you drive a car, you make a decision on the direction you will take. You are also the driver of your thoughts and have the power to decide the direction your thoughts will go in.

I remember working with a client who came to me because she was concerned, she couldn't control her thoughts. She felt that her mind was running her, rather than the other way around. This is what Buddhists call the *Monkey Mind*. Having a *Monkey Mind* means that the mind is unsettled and restless because it jumps from thought to thought like a monkey jumps from tree to tree. Don't worry, you too will cultivate the ability to tame and even program your *Monkey Mind*. Once you change your self-perception and start paying attention to your thoughts it's not as hard as you think. For now, just be willing to become aware of the thoughts that permeate your brain.

Our thoughts can be like little children running around carefree. Once a spotlight shines on them their behavior changes. That spotlight is your awareness. When you shine the light of awareness on your thoughts and pay attention to what you are thinking, your thoughts slow down. When you become aware of the thoughts you think and notice what you say to yourself, you can align your thinking to reach your desired goal.

In the *Take Action* section that follows, there are a few practices that can help quiet your mind. We begin by giving our mind something positive to focus on. Sit with the thought that your mind is a magnet that attracts people, circumstances and experiences that form the nature of your dominating thoughts. When you consciously and strategically focus the power of your mind on your primary desires, you move into alignment with the results you want to bring into your life.

> *"I don't fix problems. I fix my thinking. Then problems fix themselves."*
> *Louise Hay*

Your Thoughts Are Your Power

How many times have you wished you had more power? How many times have you wished you could change things in your life? What if I told you that you have more power than you think and believe you have? You just haven't consciously or strategically been using your power.

When you become aware of how powerful your thoughts really are, you realize how much power you already have. Once you really, really get this, you will do everything you can not to dwell in negative thoughts or to at least catch yourself when you are. Your thinking (thoughts) is your superpower.

In the last chapter, we talked about how thoughts are things. We also talked about how life uses our dominant thoughts, desires and mental images to order the things we want to manifest. When I say order, I am referring to the power of our thoughts to create our reality. Similar to how you place an order online or in a restaurant--that is the equivalent of what our thoughts do with the universe. Thoughts **are** things because every physical item our eyes see began in the form of thought-energy. It was an invisible idea first.

In the Bible, in the scripture, Proverbs 2:37 it says: *"As a man thinketh, so shall he become."* When I understood the deeper meaning of this scripture, I began to monitor my thoughts about money.

I'd been handling money based on the experiences and influences from my childhood. My ten-year-old self was running the money dialogue in my head based on inherited beliefs.

This is the equivalent of allowing an unsupervised child in a candy store. Would you let a ten-year-old manage your money?

What happens when inherited stories, money myths and archaic beliefs are allowed to run rampant in your mind? They influence the quality of your day-to-day living. You can't think poverty thoughts when you desire prosperity and money freedom.

Think of your thoughts as the blueprint for your life. Wouldn't you want to be in charge of what goes on your blueprint? We must be as selective about our thinking as we are when ordering dinner at a five-star restaurant or purchasing a new pair of shoes. Our thoughts are like a menu from which the Universe takes our order. Much like an architect draws a blueprint, the Universe turns our thoughts into tangible evidence that emerges from the quantum field.

For many years, I lived from the perspective that life was happening to me. I was the victim of the circumstances happening in my life. This relieved me of the responsibility for my actions and made what happened to me someone else's fault. This left me helpless to change my life.

When the light bulb came on, I flipped the script so I could stand in and on the power within me. This was scary at first. And even though I felt unsteady about what to do and how to do it, doing it felt like a breath of fresh air.

I encourage the people I coach to think of their mind as a computer. This makes our thoughts easier to understand. The computer analogy puts you at the helm. There you are, sitting in front of your computer (your mind). You decide what will be programmed into your code. You decide the level you want to play the game of possibilities with the Universe. You also decide what files need to be upgraded and/or deleted to achieve your goals.

You Are in a Relationship with Money

Having a healthy relationship with money is key to getting the results you desire. The requirement for having a healthy relationship with money involves not only your mindset but your feelings about money.

What does it mean to have a relationship with money? When I speak of having a relationship with money, I am referring to your thoughts and feelings about money and how they impact your money management style. The way you do or don't manage your money may be causing you frustration. Mismanaging puts you in a difficult financial position without the skills to navigate getting out of the cycle.

Reflect for a moment – how do you manage your money. Is it simply money in and payments out?

Here are some questions to help you examine your relationship with money. I encourage you to grab your journal and set aside some time over the next several days to really explore these questions and your answers.

- What spending habits do you have that create worry, anxiety and stress?

- To what degree do you feel like you can be trusted to make the highest decisions with money?
- In what ways do your money habits and thoughts move you to accomplish your goal of saving and investing to achieve financial freedom?
- How often during the month do you consult your budget for purchases?
- How easy is it for you to recognize the difference between your wants and needs?
- Do you have a financial vision for yourself and how do you foster that vision?

These are just a few questions to get you thinking more consciously about your relationship with money. Each of these actions carries an energetic blueprint. Your spending habits, your financial or prosperity vision, identifying your wants and need--all directly impact your relationship with money.

I was coaching a team member and asked her how she was handling her money. Like me, she was an entrepreneur. The more I encouraged her to evaluate her savings goals, credit card debt elimination and investing, the more I noticed her hemming and hawing, and not giving clear answers. Following my intuition, I asked her a different question, "If money was a man, what would you say about it?"

That question opened the floodgates and moved her to share.

"If my money was a man, I'd say he comes when he wants to. I can't depend on him. Once he's satisfied, he leaves quickly. He's never there when I need him. He's never enough."

Men can ask this question from the perspective of their money being a woman.

Can you relate to my client's sentiments? Clearly, she was a little frustrated in her relationship with money.

Chasing Money Like You Chase a Man or Woman

From 2013 through 2018 I invited women to explore their relationships with money through a workshop called, "Are You Chasing Money Like You Chase a Man?" Most of the women who participated had a good idea what I was attempting to convey. The focus of this workshop was on helping women become aware of their sabotaging behaviors. The analogy pointed at what happens when you chase something. The more effort and energy you expend on the chase, the further it slips away. You secretly begin to wonder if something is wrong with you. This is true about chasing men or women and true about chasing money.

My relationship with money was a mess. Our connection was wrought with anger, frustration, confusion, fear and lack of discipline. I had no direction or plan for my money. Sure, I had my checking and savings accounts, but back then my savings account was just a catchall for my checking account. Clearly, *not* a good strategy.

Every time, I'd go to my savings account thinking I had savings it would always fall short of my expectation. Without a plan, commitment or discipline to follow through, I continued to flounder like a fish out of water. I was swimming in debt and fear, not measuring up and not being responsible. Gradually I stopped damning money and being angry and disappointed with it.

As an African American woman, my money thoughts contained remnants from slavery and were passed down through generations. I hadn't considered what my own thoughts about money were. Did I like money? Was it bad to want money? If I planned to build my financial security would money corrupt me?

These were crucial questions I needed to answer because MY thoughts about money were impacting and influencing MY life and business. This is as true for you as it is for me. Your thoughts and beliefs about money have impacted and continue to impact you day-to-day which is why it's important to uncover them.

Historical Actions

Have you ever heard the story of the Thanksgiving turkey? A woman is preparing her turkey for Thanksgiving. Before she puts the turkey in the pot, she cuts the tail off. Her husband asks her why she did that. Her response is, "Because my mom does it." The son-in-law decides to ask his Mother-in-law about it at Thanksgiving dinner. When he asks her mom about it, she says, "Because my mother did it." Finally, he asks the grandmother why she cut the tail off the turkey. Her response is, "Because it didn't fit in my pan."

So, here are two generations of women, a mother and a daughter, unknowingly practicing what they saw their mother do without questioning why. This is an example of an outdated practice or unconscious belief that may not apply to a current situation. The turkey might've fit perfectly well in their pot–with the tail on.

Pause for a moment and ask yourself, in what ways are you on automatic pilot in your relationship with money? Reflect on how you manage, save or even loan your money. And let's not forget the way you pay your bills.

Are you operating from a manual filled with hand-me-down money beliefs? Have you ever stopped to question **why** they believed and did what they did and if it worked for them? If so, will it work for you in your current life experience?

This is an empowering process–to become aware of your thoughts and beliefs about money and where they originated. How many times have I heard, "Well my mom used to say …", or "My mom did…"? While it is good to take ideas from our parents, elders, and teachers that work for us, it is just as good to look deep within to find our own inner guidance, wisdom and desires. I have no doubt that there is wisdom to be gleaned from the mindset of our elders, particularly given the limited resources and opportunities that were present in their time. I can relate to them having to make ends meet when it came to prioritize the needs of the family. Fast forward to the 21st century where many people still finds themselves with the same prevailing thought of making ends meet. This saying is a reference to making food, health and money (the ends) last (or meet) until the next flow of money came in.

My mother, grandmother and aunt were all known for their ability to stretch a dollar. Eventually I learned it as well. After mismanaging the money, I received every pay day, I had to make what was left over last until my next payday.

The discipline of stretching a dollar was something I incorporated into achieving financial freedom. It took me some years to integrate that mind hack strategy to build my savings, emergency fund and move into investing.

I surpassed my parent's money saving practices. There were other lessons I needed to learn which I had to figure out on my own. My mother had talked to me about saving money but didn't talk about responsibility in spending money. In retrospect, I can see that her spending was strategically done. She would decide between shopping at the Back Room (what was formerly Loehmann's) during their private annual sales event held or buying fabric to sew me or herself a beautiful dress. My mother also spent money on Sunday dinners at Golden Bird chicken that we picked up on the way to my Grandmother Precious' house and family dinners at Clifton's Smorgasbord in downtown Los Angeles. Money in our family was also spent on rent/mortgage, food, gas and utilities.

Whether my mother had a budget or not I couldn't tell you, but she must've had some kind of accounting system because she was able to purchase two homes without credit. It's funny, when I really think about it now, my mother was a beast with money. But what I didn't get was the inside scoop of *how* she pulled it off. I would have to learn that on my own.

You Are the Cause

One of the universal principles of this planet is the *Law of Cause and Effect*. This law states that for every cause (why) there is an effect (what). You might have heard it said that for every action there is a corresponding reaction. Likewise, for every effect there is/was a cause. The effect is an event or incident that happens because of a cause.

What you may not realize, don't believe or put stock in, is YOU are the cause of the effects in your life. With the decisions we make and by the actions we do or do not take moment by moment, we cause what we experience.

This may be hard for you to grasp because it's an invisible process. We have been trained to look outside of ourselves for who we can hold responsible for what happens in our lives.

Few of us were taught that we have power over our life or what that power looks like. We look out there at *them*--the *them* is our ex-boyfriend/girlfriend, a co-worker, our mother/father, husband/wife, business partner, sister/brother as the cause. We say they make our lives difficult.

If they would make different decisions, we would be able to _____ (fill in the blank). This philosophy left me feeling like I was a victim of my circumstances and at life's whim. I lived this philosophy until my mid-thirties. My spiritual studies opened me up to a new philosophy and a broader way of looking at what happens in my life.

While this was freeing to understand, it was also frightening because accepting that I was the cause put me in the driver's seat of my life.

I wanted to stop feeling like I had darts being thrown at me all the time. It took some time for me to connect the dots. Being the cause of positive change in my life not only came with power, it came with results.

At different times of the year, throughout the United States, the weather changes and the temperature drops (the what or the cause) and slowly we notice the trees change into magnificent colors of amber, orange, brown and burgundy (the result or effect). We see these changes happening but are unaware of the unseen invisible force causing this process (in this case the seasons).

To be the cause in your life means that you control the seasons. You're the shot caller. It also means that what you think, as well as your vibration, helps manifest what shows up in your life.

No one can create a cause in your life. I used to always say, if you want to know what someone is thinking, look at their life.

Think of your mind as your creative workshop. Just as a mad scientist masterfully crafts the ingredients, creates the designs to bring ideas to life, you have the same capacity with your mind and thoughts.

If you declare and fuel the thought of having a bad day, you have unknowingly created a bad day rather than a good day or just another day to be thankful for. As bad as spilling coffee on your clothes might be it doesn't *have to* color your *entire* day unless you say so. Continuing to nurse that feeling of a bad day with your thoughts gathers more evidence to prove your point.

The universe is not going to fight you about the thoughts you hold and activate with your feelings. Our reality responds to the energy our thoughts are transmitting to the Universe. At any moment, we can shift our energy by thinking a higher thought, thus shifting the vibration being communicated to the Universe.

Some of you imagine winning the lottery. It's one thing to think about winning the lottery. It's another thing to think thoughts energetically aligned with what you want and desire. Thinking about winning the lotto might not make it happen but it can and will connect with the energy of abundance.

You can think anything you consciously choose. However, if you recognize yourself as the cause, you understand the importance of thinking thoughts that are aligned with your desired results. This process can be described by a quote I heard many years ago and never forgot.

The quote is from Rev. Dr. Johnnie Colemon, founder of *Christ Universal Temple* in Chicago, Illinois. Rev. Dr. Colemon founded *Christ Universal Temple* in 1956 and was a pioneer in the *New Thought* movement. In 2006 she created her own denomination, the *Universal Foundation for Better Living.* Her quote was simply:

"You are the thinker who thinks the thoughts that creates the things in your life."

I love this quote. It teaches us about our inherent power. And that from the simple and power-filled act of thinking positively, we can manifest the things in our lives that we really want.

There's Just Not Enough Money

Another step in developing a healthy relationship with money happened when I begin to question the overall notion that there wasn't enough money in the world.

The idea that there is scarcity with money--there's only so much. This is the world view that strangles so many of us. The belief that the rich get richer and the poor get poorer speaks to this. The justification for our financial woes stems from the belief that there isn't enough money to go around.

For many years I believed this untruth. Actually, I had more than enough money. What I didn't have was the mindset, knowledge and commitment to manage my money effectively.

Unfortunately, many you have found comfort in thinking this is the reason for your past or present experiences. It's easy to use the excuse that there's isn't enough to go around. So many people experience financial lack that it's easy to believe we are among them.

We are spiritual beings living in a physical form. The spiritual aspect of us is energy and transmits a vibrational frequency. Quantum physics, science and spirituality have joined together to reveal that there is a powerful partnership within each of us that we activate through our thoughts. As spiritual beings, we are forever connected to the universal energy of all life at our core. We have a body, but we are not limited by our body because we are not only physical in form. Since the universe is infinite, as is energy, then everything is infinite.

It All Starts with a Thought

How does this happen you ask? Brilliantly! What we have learned from quantum physics is that everything is energy and energy is invisible. This includes our thoughts which are also invisible. And energy vibrates at a certain frequency.

We talked earlier in the book about the story of the house someone wants to build and live in. It started with an idea. From the idea, we enlisted the skills of an architect. Then we hired a contractor to bring the vision of the house into physical

115

form. What this emphasizes is that everything we manifest begins within.

Look more closely at life as you move through it. Notice that everything you see was once someone's idea held in the invisible aspect of life.

This process is also displayed in nature. Take for example the journey of the caterpillar transforming into a butterfly. It's the very same journey we take. Everything we see, touch and taste was once an invisible idea that was brought to life. This energy, transforming ideas into reality, is etched within our being. This energy coursing through our veins is our essence. It is our energetic DNA.

Have you written a book or created a top selling product? Have you had a fundraising idea that you organized, planned on paper, hired a team and brought to manifestation? Have you created a program for your church or community? Maybe you developed a new App, a fashion line, designed a piece of jewelry or created a soul-stirring musical piece. Whatever we do, everything comes through us from the inside (thought) out.

Let's go back to the house example. The house was once the homeowner's dream but has now manifested into a real, tangible object. Think about the table we use, the chairs we sit on, the cars we drive, everything came from within to the outside. Think about Steve Jobs who created Apple or Mark Zuckerberg who created Facebook. Their mega successes began with a single thought!

You're Only Using 10% of Your Power

117

Most people are trained to only use their conscious mind. The conscious mind is 10% of who we are and 10% of our true power. This 10% is good for basic things like paying bills, navigating traffic, managing household responsibilities, running a business or going to work, etc. What do you do with the other 90% of your power that is not being used? To illustrate this, think of an iceberg.

You're familiar with seeing the tip of the iceberg jutting out of the water. But there is considerably more of the iceberg beneath the surface. It's the same for everyone. When you only use your conscious thinking mind, you're just accessing the tip of the iceberg. That leaves the other 90% that is not being used. The 90% is your gold mine of possibilities being stored beneath the surface.

Let's revisit a question I posed earlier in the book. I asked readers how can two people working at the same place of employment, in the same position, with the same income live completely different lifestyles? The answer: it's their mindset. The thoughts, beliefs and relationships they have with money.

A New Thought About Money

"Choose your thoughts carefully. You are the masterpiece of your life." The Secret

I was doing all I knew to stay afloat and dodge the bullets life sometimes sends our way. As I prepared to teach my spiritual congregation a new perspective about money and infinite prosperity, I explored the truth of what I really believed and thought about money.

I had shifted my perspectives and was excited to teach my parishioners new principles on wealth and prosperity. But it occurred to me that I needed to first get them and you who are reading this book, to evaluate their own beliefs.

Do you think that the only way to have money is to work hard? Do you still subscribe to the thinking that the rich get richer and the poor get poorer? These are some of the unconscious negative thoughts we carry into our relationship with money.

Here's a little secret. Each of these thoughts is based on the worldview of scarcity and lack which is a lie. Also, the energy of these thoughts sends out vibrations in a frequency that will not attract what you desire.

When you began reading this book, you may not have known how powerful you and your thoughts were. Or you knew and didn't know how the two worked together.

It is important that we look at money with joy and consider it an object of exchange. I think of money as an outward, external representation of something that is far bigger than the piece of paper it is printed on. For me, money is directly connected to the Infinite Source. It comes to us through many different outlets such as jobs, investments, businesses, inheritances, income taxes and gifts. There is only one infinite source of abundance and prosperity is an offspring of it.

There's nothing on the planet that didn't start as a spark from within. You may have a problem accepting this if you hold subconscious thoughts and beliefs that keep your energy around money at a low vibrational frequency.

To understand the vibrational frequency of your thoughts about money, consider which of these thoughts resonate for you?

- When I think of money, I get sad.
- Money doesn't come when I need it.
- Money comes easy but it doesn't stay.
- Money is effortless sometimes.
- Money comes and then I need to fix something.

This list shows us how money gets a bad rap when it is merely an inanimate object without thoughts or feelings.

Before becoming an entrepreneur, I always had a 9-to-5 job. As a licensed clinical social worker, I also had the option of working a side gig. When I wanted or needed more money, I got another job.

At one point, I had my 9-to-5 job, my spiritual congregation and my private practice. I worked seven days a week following the storyline, "I work hard for the money." But at the end of the day, I didn't necessarily have that much more money. Why was that?

The reason: I didn't change anything about how I managed, thought or felt about money.

What about you? Has it worked for you to have a job and side gig? Are you successful at managing the additional money you make? Did you start with a specific plan? Have you gotten off track? Have you paid off one of your credit cards or contributed to your savings account regularly? Or is the extra money you earn what some call, *play money*? Consider ways to better manage the money you have, rather than adding another hour of work to your already full schedule.

I didn't know that the source of my prosperity was within me or even connected to me. I focused all of my effort outwardly. We must become more intentional about our thoughts. *Money Mastery Now* helps us summon the courage to create new beliefs rather than hold onto inherited thoughts and beliefs that no longer serve us.

It Takes Too Much Work

You might think the process in this book is a lot of work. I get it. For some of you these are new ideas. For others, it's a refresher leading to your next step. Your first impulse might be to push back or resist the information you are being called to embrace. It's not unusual to be hesitant about changing the way we manage money.

Take this opportunity to pause your reading and pull out your journal. Revisit your goals. Revisit WHY you want to live in financial freedom and prosperity.

When finished, consider these questions. On a scale of one to ten how would you rate the amount of time you spend on the following. To make it simple 1 represents the least amount of time, 5 equal time and 10 maximum time. You'll write this in your journal.

- How much time, and energy do you spend worrying about money? Write that number in your journal. (Either a 1 for not much, 5 for enough and 10 for the worry money loop.)
- How much energy does it take for you to fuss, fret and feel secretly frazzled about money? Write that number in your journal.
- How much time do you engage in self-criticism, disappointment and shaming for not keeping your word to yourself? Write that number in your journal.
- How much time do you spend comparing yourself to others, be it your siblings or friends?
- How much wear and tear does this entire process take on your physical body? Think about the quantity of sleepless nights vs. the

nights you slept well. Write that number in your journal.

Now, look at how many 10's you have and how many 5's. What was the total?

Doesn't that seem like a lot of energy?

Many live with various degrees of inherited family stories, beliefs and lies. We also have our own misguided thoughts. Over time this way of living becomes familiar.

Human nature wants us to be comfortable and to find a familiar place in our uncomfortableness. But look where being comfortable has gotten you as it relates to your money and financial goals.

Let me share one of my favorite stories that illustrates this point. It comes from Les Brown, one of the top motivational speakers in the country and one of my speaking mentors. He tells the story about a dog on a porch.

There was an elderly couple sitting in rocking chairs on their porch. A young man walked by the house and noticed a moaning dog lying between the couple. The young man walked by the next day and again noticed the couple sitting on the porch rocking in their chairs while their dog moaned in pain.

The young man told himself that if the dog was moaning the next day when he walked by, he would ask the couple what was wrong with the dog. Sure enough, as he walked by the next day, the dog was moaning. The young man asked the woman what was wrong with the dog. She said, "Oh, he's lying on a nail. It hurts him enough to moan about it but not enough to move."

From this story, we learn how we can be engaged in self-imposed torture. The dog preferred to lay there moaning than to get up and off of the nail.

We must pay attention to how we harness the power of our thoughts or let our monkey mind run amuck. We also must assess and determine if we are moving closer to or further from financial freedom. If we complain about our situation but do nothing to improve it, we are just like the dog lying on the nail.

Your Mind Is Your Computer

Envision your mind as a high-powered PC that is connected to a Mother Board. You are in control of inputting data and installing programs on health, relationships, goals, religion, travel, philanthropy and dreams into this computer.

What happens when your computer hardware is outdated and can't accept the newest software?

If this happened to your desktop, you would simply install the newest version of the program. When you think of your mind like a computer, you know that to stay up to speed, you must update your software regularly. Otherwise you might end up working with outdated information. If this is true about computers, why wouldn't you update the programs and data stored in your thoughts and beliefs file?

You are the only one who can update your personal computer. You do so by installing a newer, updated program into your thoughts. With these thoughts, you can create a new reality, or you can continue to fuel the reality you are currently living.

"Training and managing your own mind are the most important skill you could ever own in terms of both your happiness and your success." T. Harv Eker

As stated earlier in the book, it's hard to attract money when most of your money thoughts are along these lines:

- It's selfish to have or want money.
- The rich get richer and the poor get poorer.
- Money is the root of all evil.
- Money is exhausting.

Money doesn't stand a chance with these thoughts. No matter the desired outcome, whether it is $100k of revenue in your business, creating prosperous business partnerships, eliminating credit card debt or investing in real estate. You will struggle to achieve results unless you install new thoughts and train your mind to focus on thoughts that are aligned with your desired outcome.

You can't hold thoughts of generating $100k in revenue in your business and focus thought energy on the ways you can't do it. You want to save money or eliminate credit card debt, but your accompanying thought is that it's too hard.

You're literally thinking a thought that is totally opposite of your desire. I describe this as attempting to sit down and stand up at the same time.

You train your mind for the results you desire. Remember it's your computer. You give your mind the script. You tell it what you want it to think. This isn't about you working harder. It is about training your mind to work smarter.

132

You're Only Using 10% of Your Power

Most people are trained to only use their conscious mind. The conscious mind is 10% of who we are and 10% of our true power. This 10% is good for basic things like paying bills, navigating traffic, managing household responsibilities, running a business or going to work, etc. What do you do with the other 90% of your power that is not being used? To illustrate this, think of an iceberg.

You're familiar with seeing the tip of the iceberg jutting out of the water. But there is considerably more of the iceberg beneath the surface. It's the same for everyone. When you only use your conscious thinking mind, you're just accessing the tip of the iceberg. That leaves the other 90% that is not being used. The 90% is your gold mine of possibilities being stored beneath the surface.

Let's revisit a question I posed earlier in the book. I asked readers how can two people working at the same place of employment, in the same position, with the same income live completely different lifestyles? The answer: it's their mindset. The thoughts, beliefs and relationships they have with money.

TAKE ACTION

This next exercise is designed to help you step into your power and think conscious thoughts to intentionally align your words with the results you desire.

1. First, be patient with yourself. The key to this process is to become present and aware of your thoughts about money

throughout the day. Become an observer of your inner dialogue while in the store, making purchases, paying bills and invoices. Pay attention to your thoughts while grocery shopping, investing, making loans to others, investing in your health and/or during your personal development.

2. Next decide on a week when you will intentionally track your thoughts each day. Use your journal to write down what you hear yourself say.

3. Set aside time each night to review your thoughts about money.

4. Take a sheet of paper and draw a line down the center of the page. At the top of the left side write THOUGHT. On the right side of the page draw two more lines to create three columns. Label the

135

first column SOURCE, the second column TRUTH, and the third column QUALITY.

It should look like this:
Thought | Source | Truth | Quality

5.   Write all of the thoughts you heard yourself say in the THOUGHT column.

6.   Then take some time to identify the original source of each thought. Once you identify the source write it in the SOURCE column next to the thought.

7.   Then ask yourself if you believe this and if so, why? Add a "T" or "F" to the TRUTH column to indicate if you consider this your truth.

8.   In the QUALITY column indicate the quality or vibration of this

thought. Is it historical, inherited or a personally created thought?

9. Reflect on each one of the thoughts for one week to determine if it is moving you toward your goals.

10. To reflect on a new thought, write it on a 3x5 card and take it into your morning meditation or intention setting time. Recite this thought to yourself throughout the day. Stand in front of a mirror and repeat the thought to yourself while looking in your eyes. Notice how it feels to hold this thought about money or your goal. Is there a smidgen of excitement for the possibility of this truth? Is there a tickle or tingle on some internal level that calls you to live day-to-day from this perspective?

This is actually what a thought is – a perspective you hold about a subject or item. When that thought is of high energy it will transmit that vibrational frequency into the universe and connect with matching and aligned vibrations. The purpose of the transmission is to return to you what you are vibrating.

Think of it like trying on a new pair of shoes. You put them on and walk around in them. Then you look at them in the mirror. You might walk around in them several more times paying attention to how they feel before you say yes. Think of this example when considering your thoughts.

Just as you wouldn't pay top dollar for a pair of uncomfortable shoes, you don't want to ignite a thought that doesn't feel good or is not

aligned with your ultimate goals and
desires.

Chapter Three-Align Your

Words – Design

or Default

"In the beginning was the Word."

Words consist of sound and vibration. These vibrations create the reality of our lives. Words themselves are the creators of our lives. Without words our thoughts could never become reality. Even though you may not think of it this way, your words are the tools you use to create.

When I started my healing journey, I began to recognize the power of my words. In certain experiences in my life I felt that I was a victim. I was taught by my mom that my smart mouth led to some of my painful and difficult consequences.

This demonstrated an external response to my words. I still hadn't made the connection between my words and what showed up in my life as a direct result of what I said. I ask this question to my readers: are you speaking from design or default?

What do I mean by speaking from design or default? I'm glad you asked. When you speak by design you are consciously aware of the words you say. That awareness includes understanding that each word or sentence carries its own power to impact your energetic vibration. For example, think of positive affirmations that you have intentionally crafted. With these affirmations, you have spoken words for a specific result. This is an example of speaking by design. This is the power that your words have to shape your perceptions that in turn shape your thoughts, beliefs, behaviors and life.

Likewise, when you speak from default (fear, worry, doubt), you are unconsciously using the power of your words against yourself. You know this, to a degree, but for many of us it is unconscious. When you say things to yourself like, *I'm so stupid* or *I never get things right* you are silently speaking judgment against yourself and your heart. These words become the perceptions that manifest as your thoughts, behaviors and beliefs about yourself.

It's not just the words, it's their implication. Speaking sentences such as, "I'll never get out of debt" or "If I don't loan money to my family, they'll be mad at me," falsely indicate powerlessness to escape to freedom from debt. You also tell the universe that you have no value beyond what you do for others. With each unconscious word you move yourself out of alignment with what is possible.

How many of us grew up hearing the rhyme, *sticks and stones may break my bones, but words will never hurt me*?" That has proven to be untrue. Words do hurt. Words spoken in anger, hate and fear can cause great pain. We all remember something someone said to us that hurt our feelings. While we do have the power to heal our hearts from hurtful words, let us first acknowledge that words can strike a painful, personal blow.

Let's look at how the words we speak impact (hurt) our money and our relationship with money.

144

Here's some of the words I've heard people say over the years – first about money and second, about themselves – as it relates to money.

- *Money burns a hole in my pocket.*
- *Money is hard work.*
- *Money never comes when I need it.*
- *There is never enough money to go around.*
- *Money isn't that important.*
- *I'm a failure.*
- *I'm not good with money, I'm so dumb.*
- *I didn't handle the money in my marriage. I'm not smart enough to figure it out.*
- *I wasn't taught how to manage money.*
- *Money comes and money goes.*

Do any of these resonate with you?

Your Words Matter

Now understanding the tremendous power of our words, it's time to use them to help not hurt our financial life. Our words can help reshape our material world. The words we speak can pull us together uniting us or create greater divisions. Even with our children, words between parents with different parenting styles, can divide and create a family riff. Think of your own family and the words that pulled you together or divided you.

We've all had an experience of hearing an inspirational message that lifted our spirit, ignited us with joy and moved us into action. It is through the power of words that ideas are planted. How we perceive ourselves, our potential, how we show up in the world and in our life.

What you say, how you say it and when you say it matters. I remember teaching myself to speak to be heard versus blowing off steam or being reckless with my words. What I desired was to communicate my thoughts and feelings and let my words be heard. I had to learn to speak in way that brought that goal to fruition.

From the words, *I love you* to silently telling ourselves *we're not good enough*. Or hearing a compliment, "I like the suit you're wearing," and not pausing to take that in. Even saying, "I'm not happy," can increase the power of that feeling.

Many know firsthand the power of our words in loving moments as well as in heated disagreements. Likewise, we have learned how difficult it is to take back our words. While I'll dive into this subject in the next chapter, I want to include here the element that fuels our words and gives them a punch...it's our feelings.

In conclusion, recognize that words can bring you into alignment with what you desire. Conversely, our words can also move us out of alignment with what we seek to attract. When we don't recognize the power of our words, we may use them in ways that nullify our efforts to achieve our goals.

Take a moment and grab your journal. I'll wait. You have it? Ponder the following questions and write down your realizations in your journal.

- What is it that has you awake in the middle of the night when you desperately long to close your eyes and get some sleep? Do you lay there with your imaginary calculator attempting to make the numbers between your expenses and your earnings match?

- Do you often speak from a place of lack, scarcity or not enough? Or maybe you speak from hope rather than assurance, confidence or prosperity. Are you frequently complaining, silently judging yourself and your spending habits or just living moment to moment in worry and stress?

If you answered yes to any of the above, you are robbing yourself of the very thing you seek to create in your life. Don't feel bad about this truth. Instead, start taking note of your words today. Accept the power of your words and begin using them as an instrument to create the life, experience, marriage, relationship, business and happiness you desire and deserve.

I was taught that you couldn't get into the Kingdom of Heaven with a lot of money. Yet the church was asking for financial contributions three times in the morning service alone. My ability to embrace the prosperity that surrounded me happened when I took responsibility for my relationship with money and the words I spoke about money as a whole.

Speak Over Your Money

In modern society, there is a tendency to talk about what's not working. People regularly complain about problems and circumstances. Many do this commiserating thing with our friends, not consciously thinking about what we are communicating to the universe. There is an old saying, "Choose your words wisely." When we recognize ourselves as the creators of our lives and our words as the instrument of creation, we understand that harnessing the power of our words can produce powerful results.

I've discovered that money is not a subject widely and openly discussed, even among friends. I credit this lack of discussion to the shame we feel around our mismanaging money. We keep our financial challenges a secret for fear of judgement. We withdraw, all the while looking good on the outside while struggling on the inside. We are literally hiding in plain sight.

I cried, complained and worried. And oh boy, did I pray! It was all in vain, because my vibrational frequency was so low and filled with fear. I've come to know that we can't desire prosperity while focusing on poverty. It's not a vibrational match.

Let's look at some of the common statements and check their vibrational match to see which statements are aligned and those that aren't.

- *Money is my friend. (Aligned?)*
- *Money never comes when I need it. (Aligned to attract money?)*
- *I never seem to have enough money. (High vibrational frequency?)*
- *This is too expensive.*
- *Money comes to me easily.*
- *I'll never be able to afford that.*
- *Money and I just don't get along.*

Money Mastery consciousness won't work if we speak affirming statements like, *I desire more money* and then complain that *the rich get richer while the poor get poorer.*

When you've grown up in a family that struggled financially you were probably taught that there would never be enough money. This inherited language and belief system might've been passed down from your family, church or your culture. Thinking this way can derail your efforts to align with the missing link to having more than enough money.

Money Mastery Now calls you to accept the power of your words to create. When you consciously choose words that align with your goals, this triggers changes in your relationship with money which produce tangible results in your bank account.

I imagine some of you are thinking, "Is that all I have to do – choose my words?" Well, think of it as a starting place. Your vibrational frequency is the invisible signal you send to the universe through your words. This is the signal that you want to align with to accomplish what you desire.

Vibrational Frequency of Words

I've shared that words have layers. On one layer, we use them to communicate. On another layer, they are energy and have a vibrational frequency. We always feel our words, sometimes unconsciously.

We may be more familiar with words that feel good or hurtful but there are so many levels in between. Words contain energy and possess power. When we're present to them, we can feel the difference in the energy of them.

Can you remember a time when you felt the vibrational frequency of someone's words? I was recently reminded of it when I felt my heart being pierced by a statement a dear friend of mine made. The words themselves were on one level but the vibrational frequency of the them was so sharp I remember feeling like a dart had been shot through my heart. Several days later, I reflected on the experience and was so amazed by the energy and power of words. It's funny, there were many things my mother said to me when she was alive, but her statement, "You're not going to amount to anything" still echoes in my memory. Did it hurt? Of course, it did.

What I realized was that her words triggered an anger within me and unknowingly that anger was a quiet fuel for me to prove her wrong.

What about you? Can you remember such a moment in your life? If so, then you know the power of the vibrational frequency of words. The key awareness here is that words vibrate at different frequencies which affect us.

One of my favorite books is *Power vs Force* by the enlightened teacher, David R. Hawkins. This is a highly recommended read that will help you learn about energy and more importantly, how to stop trying to force things to happen. Hawkins' book offers a numerical indicator for the vibrational frequency of humans. 500 is the highest vibrational frequency. The average person's indicator is 200.

Hawkins also talks about how the word and the feeling of love has the highest vibrational energy at 500. He also points out that for many of us, our frequency is too low for what we desire in our lives. That's when I understood the importance of aligning our thoughts, words and feelings to attract what we desire to accomplish.

It's not enough to simply read this book and put it away. But as you complete the exercises throughout the book, you will begin to make a shift. You'll also start to recognize the language, habits and actions you have inherited that are robbing you of financial freedom. Awareness is the key to changing behavior. What you are aware of can influence and align you with your desired results.

Are you ready?

Grab your journal and become present and alert to the energy of your words throughout the day. What words do you hear and how do they make you feel? Which words trigger a smile within you, or which words trigger sadness?

Take one day and begin to notice how words hold you and make you feel. This practice is to help you learn to communicate with the universe and align with your goals.

Think of the word *soft*? What comes to mind? What feelings or images pop up for you with this word?

Now think about the word *hard*? How does that energy feel? Can you feel the difference between the words?

We actually feel the energy of words. Try it for yourself. Think of the word tall and then short.

Does the energy of the word tall feel more expansive or spacious? What about the energy of the word short? Does it feel smaller or lower to the ground? Interesting, right?

Even with words that don't seem to have an emotional value, we still feel a difference between them. Because words have energy.

One example to think of is the vibration of prayer. When I was growing up my mom, grandmother, aunt and myself, attended *Tabernacle of Faith Baptist Church*. This was the church of my birth. There was an elder minister who used a powerful prayer. We teased him about the slowness of his prayer.

By the time I was a teenager, the power of his words resonated with me. He was Reverend George Campbell and his prayer always began with three words spoken in reverence. Those three words suggested a power within us that was intimate and deeply personal. This was a power I did not know in my youth but would come to know quite well. The words he said were simple but the feeling, the vulnerability of his acknowledgement was equivalent of a man bowing his head to God. It reminded me of what is done in the mosque five times a day to summon Muslims to worship.

His words were, "God (with a reverent one-minute pause), Our Father."

The vibration of those three words-- God, our Father–still resonates with me today. Reverend Campbell's prayer felt so personal and intimate. It was as if he were peeking into a man's sacred moment with God. That is the vibrational frequency that was palpable to me. And I have no doubt that his prayer held a high vibrational frequency in the Universe.

For some of you it may be prayer and for others, it may be chanting or singing. It could be the stillness of meditation. All of these energies transmit a vibrational frequency to the Universe giving it one option--and that is to return that vibration to its creator-YOU. The vibrational frequency you send out speaks to the lightness, joy, expansiveness, alignment and freedom you communicate to the Universe.

The lighter the energy of your words, the higher your frequency is with the Universe. Be sure to explore the Instrument Panel in the Resources section of the book to download your personal guide.

Your physical body works in tandem with your spiritual/energetic body. Your spiritual/energetic body is made of the same substance as the universe thus the two are always in communication. Take a moment and connect the dots to the power of words in your life. What you say out loud and what you harbor within is what you will experience.

Some of us tap into this power every day when we sing songs while driving, walking or working out. There is a vibration associated with each word we use and how we use it.

Think of how your intention is conveyed through your words when you speak to a young child, a good friend, your parents or a bill collector. Notice how the words from a compliment make you feel or the words from your work evaluation or the words you read in a card of appreciation feel.

We are bombarded with words all day from the television, radio, workplace, gas station, hair salon, gym, grocery stores, etc. There is no place where words are not being used. Take some time today and be present to how the words you hear make you feel and how they impact you throughout the day.

Think about the all-day news stations--that's a good one. How do those words make you feel and impact your vibrational frequency? Or the words on social media–how do they make you feel when you read them?

Oh, and here's a good one. Ladies, what about all those songs you sing that you know word for word and sing with just as much, if not more intensity, than the singer. Take a moment and notice which songs and words are in alignment with what you desire in your relationships.

Notice how the words feel and what their energetic vibration feels like to you. My goal is for you to become more present to the words in your life, as well as be present to the words you speak, and see if they are a vibrational match for your desires.

Your Money Language

Just as we speak into our life and heart moment-by-moment, we bring the same power of words to the language we use in our relationship with money.

I didn't have a clue about the power of my complaining, worrying and shaming myself in my relationship with money. First of all, I didn't think of it as a relationship and second, in the beginning I didn't know there was a missing link. I figured if I worked harder, I'd get more results. So, that's what I did.

No one would ever say I didn't work hard for what I wanted. Yet, my best efforts didn't produce better results and if anything, added to my frustration.

I had a connection to Spirit and God but based on what I'd been taught in my youth, God and money couldn't coexist. I didn't have anyone to talk to about the beliefs about money I had inherited. In my family, you didn't talk about money. The conversations I did hear were usually my mother fussing at my dad about his gambling.

I encourage readers to take a moment and survey the history of your money language and what you secretly tell yourself about it. Write about it in your journal with the understanding that this practice will be part of the work you do to transform your relationship with money.

So, you don't feel alone, I'd like to share a guided meditation I use to help women in my coaching program tap into their true feelings about money. These are some of their statements in response to the meditation with money:

- What took you so long?

- I know you're not going to stay long.

- You never come when I need you.

- How long are you going to stay this time?

- Welcome, come have a seat.

And while this last one isn't the exact words used, it is the action one woman took in anger and frustration with money. When money showed up – she said she simply…"Closed the door in money's face."

Our level of frustration with money can be overwhelming. And it's unfortunate we feel that way because money is totally innocent.

I no longer blame money or hold it responsible for my woes. Years ago, I learned to focus on my irresponsibility with the money I *did* have. I figured it wasn't money's fault, because in truth, even back then, I had enough money. Heck, I was working seven days a week! I just didn't have the money skills, confidence, knowledge or support to make strategic decisions to maximize the benefits of the money I had.

Hang in there. Hang in there for yourself like you do for everyone else. You are worth it. Your dreams and desires are worth it too.

When you finish this book and after you complete the exercises, you'll begin to uncover the thoughts and words that are interfering with your positive results. My hope is learned to fight for yourself and be willing to create new patterns, language and ways of being in relationship with money. Today is the day you take a few more steps toward actualizing your Money Mastery. Let's go!

Here's another way you can discover your money language. Think about what you say to your children when they ask you to buy something. How do you feel when your child asks you for something and you have to say no?

Grab your journal and write down your responses. Cultivate the practice of feeling the energy of the words you speak.

Why is this so important?

Partly because many of us are on automatic pilot when it comes to our relationship with money. We use the same low vibration language over and over, which doesn't match what we desire. This exercise is simply for you to be present to your language. I think it was James Baldwin who said, "We can't change what we can't see." This exercise is about you seeing, in writing, what you are speaking (and of course feeling) about money.

Discover the words you use most when speaking about your money. Notice if you wrap your money in words of lack, anger, disappointment or frustration. In the end, you'll have a list of words that describe your current relationship with money.

Next, create an up-to-date list of the words that align you with financial

169

relief, peace of mind, confidence and possibility.

For example, if your word list looks like: "Money makes me sick." You need to upgrade your communication to the Universe. The more you're able to align your thoughts and beliefs around money the closer you'll be to the results you desire and deserve.

Speaking Truth

Let me say again that words consist of two parts: visible and invisible. The first part (visible) is sound and the second part (invisible) is vibration. Many women center their interactions with one another around problems, adversities, worries, doubts and fear. We seek solace and even a sense of relief from thinking we're in it all alone. But what we don't realize is that the words we joke about are connected to deeper feeling.

Each word we speak gives power to what will become our reality. I remember the, "I'm so broke I could" joke. That phrase became a comedic competition to prove who was the most broke. I never thought there was anything funny about not having money.

Some of you may be saying, "My truth is that I *am* broke." To that I say, being financially challenged is temporary. It's not a life sentence. When your money is short, it can feel like it will be that way forever. Here's the caveat, if we keep speaking the broke energy into our finances, we could energetically lock ourselves into that moment. Speaking what we desire can create that reality in our lives. We must shift our focus to what we want rather than lamenting on what is currently happening.

I encourage women to talk to each other about money in ways that fuels our common goals. Sharing the challenges can help us make strategic decisions for ourselves and our families and feel confident doing so.

Recognize the true power of your voice and your spoken words to the Universe. Become more conscious about using your superpower.

Take all that energy, all that talking you do--and you know you can talk--and laser focus it on positive thoughts about money. That conversation will move you in the direction of fulfilling your hopes and dreams.

The power of your spoken words cannot be understated. Your

acceptance of the power of your words is critical to manifesting visible results in your life, business and bank account.

When you say something out loud repetitively, fueled by passionate feelings, it has the potential to become your truth. When you embrace the truth that words create your reality, you understand the importance of aligning your words with stated desires.

You are the Creator in your universe. As the creator of your life, the first way to align with money is through your thoughts.

PRACTICE

- For one week, document the most common words you hear yourself say in relation to your money.

- Notice the energy and vibration of your words. Ask yourself, are these words aligned with my goals? If not, what words would be aligned? Try those words on for size to up-level your word uses about money.

- Create at least five statements that consciously align with your desired results.

Chapter Four-Align Your Feelings–Your Feelings Matter, Too

The truth of the matter is that money is all about your emotions and your feelings. Jenenne Macklin

What makes your words so powerful is the fuel behind them. That fuel is your feelings and emotions. With each word, there is a conscious or unconscious realization. This makes it clear that feelings and emotions transmit a vibrational frequency.

Without awareness of your feelings and how they determine your decisions and actions, you might think you're using logic when you're not.

Also, if you rely solely on your head, you access only 10% of your power, while denying the other 90%.

Unfortunately, many of us have been programmed to distrust our feelings. From disappointing break-ups and divorces, family loss, betrayal by close friends--not trusting our heart could've protected us from a lot of pain. Not trusting our heart may've worked in the early years but the older we get not trusting can hurt us. Actually, it didn't work in the early years, we just told ourselves it did.

We all experience hurt as part of our journey here on earth. But that isn't a good reason not to trust the wisdom of our heart. What I've learned from my journey and from coaching and mentoring women, is that usually when we feel hurt it's because we ignored the flashing red lights.

Instead, we sashay right into the lights telling ourselves, "I'll make it work." We ignore the subtle tap on the shoulder, the glaring warning signs and the three-alarm sirens. We find ourselves hurt, disappointed, feeling betrayed, alone, and at times, abandoned. That's been my experience and the experience of many of my clients. When we trust the wisdom that comes from within and act accordingly, more often than not we will recover our happy.

Feelings are a fundamental part of the very fabric of the Universe we live in. Trusting our feelings, intuition and first mind is an acknowledgment of our inner wisdom. It also acknowledges the direct, divine information that exists to support our success.

We've all walked through some difficult experiences. We've risen to the top, fallen down, laid down, crawled or maybe even been kicked down and still gotten up to rise again. Each experience we've been through carries within it a nugget of wisdom. When we recognize the wisdom nuggets, they offer insights into ourselves and our behavior. They also provide clarity of past or present events and what we should've done different.

Wisdom nuggets connect the dots of our life experiences. These show up as subtle feelings, hunches, flashes of insight, first mind whispers and at times screaming pain. They guide us toward our goals and away from distractions that aren't aligned with our goals and desired results.

Embrace the fast track to clarity and to transmit an aligned vibrational frequency. This is the system of the Universe. This is the energy we are made out of and are part of.

We are not only physical beings--we are energetic beings. *Money Mastery Now* calls us to recognize all of who we are, not just our tangible, physical aspects.

We must employ the highest words possible when speaking about money. Let each word we speak be infused with passion and a vibrational frequency that positively communicates to the universe.

I Deserve It

The impromptu vacation you took, the real estate purchase you made or the clothes you bought, did you recognize that you deserved it?

I remember speaking to a group of women at the Guidance Church in Los Angeles. There was a delightful conversation with a woman who had purchased a dress. I asked her what made her make the purchase.

She said she bought the dress because the store clerk told her she looked good in it. After laughing, I told her, "That was her job!" I also explained that though the salesperson encouraged her to make the purchase, the decision to do so came from within. Then I dug a little deeper...

I asked her, "What did you tell yourself to make it okay to make the purchase?" The room was quiet. I waited patiently for her answer. She had to think about her feelings and what she told herself. She said softly, "I deserved it."

She told herself she deserved it even though she had not gone into the store intending to make a purchase. She told herself she deserved it because it was a special event and it was on sale. The woman also revealed that she bought the dress because she felt a little overweight and wanted to look nice for an event. That answer brought a powerful conclusion to the discussion. What energy was really, unconsciously, spending her money?

What Do My Feelings Have to Do with It?

Let me be clear--your feelings are the fuel for your vibration. When you understand this, you get how reckless and unconscious spending impacts your feelings about yourself. From that spur of the moment $10,000 purchase that is triggered because you don't feel heard or loved by your spouse, to the clothes you buy and hide in the back of the closet, feelings are the trigger. Couple this with the fact that your feelings are the fuel for your vibration (your communication to the Universe), and you may be able to understand how your underlying feelings can lead to spontaneous purchases. I find this especially in my coaching work with women. Women are much more likely to jeopardize plans to save and become financially solvent. Unconscious spending jeopardizes our goal of financial ease.

On a deeper level, overspending can feel like self-betrayal. We've broken a promise to ourselves to save a certain amount. Now we've made an unplanned purchase that wasn't in our budget.

I'm not saying you don't deserve whatever you want to buy. What I'm saying is that if it's not in your budget, you don't deserve it *right now.* It's not more important than achieving your financial goal.

I suggest you set some time aside to check what's going on inside your heart. Are you hurt, disappointed, lonely, feeling invisible or unappreciated? In your quiet time, spend some time with this experience. Uncover negative feelings you might be caring and then let it pass.

Exploring underlying issues like insecurities about weight can reveal the core reasons for impulse spending. Honoring your worth and value on the planet will too.

Your Personal GPS

Many of us weren't taught that our feelings are valuable. This makes sense because many of us in the United States aren't taught to value ourselves. For some women, there is a tendency to push our feelings aside and trust our head because it's not as indecisive as our heart. I'd say we have it backwards.

Our feelings are the most advanced navigational equipment within us. An epic book called, *Law of Attraction* by Esther and Jerry Hicks, confirms this idea. In *Law of Attraction*, Esther channels the energy of her spirit guide, *Abraham.* The book also offers spiritual insights and guidance. I attended several of their personal appearances and found them extremely powerful. In the teachings from Esther and Abraham, Abraham considers our feelings to be our emotional guidance. Following are a few quotes from their bestselling book. Write them on your mirror, recite them throughout the day and reflect on how they make you feel.

- *Life is treating you as you feel.*

- *The greatest gift you can ever give another person is your own happiness.*

- *Your feelings attract what you experience.*

- *Nothing is more important than feeling good.*

Feelings can warn us, energize us, ignite our creativity and passion. Feelings can also stir our sexual and sensual flames and sparks the flame of jealousy, faith, anger, fear and lust. Recognizing the power of your feelings can be the key to your financial freedom. Feelings are one of the highest vibrational frequencies you can transmit to Source.

Feeling your feelings can be a great relief. I remember thinking that I didn't have time to get caught up in my feelings because I had so much to do. Some of you might find it easy to share your feelings. Others may have a hard time honoring and respecting what goes on inside.

Emotional Guidance Systems

I have studied and relied on insights from experts, coaches and teachers such as Dr. David Hawkins, Esther and Jerry Hicks with the teaching of Abraham. I also got a great deal from my dear friend Lola Jones' teachings of Divine Openings.

Dr. David Hawkins uses a calibration scale called the *Scale of Human*

186

Consciousness that reveals a numeric score for our vibrational frequency. It can be found in his book, *Power vs Force: The Hidden Determinants of Human Behavior.* Esther and Jerry Hicks (Abraham) offer what they call an *Emotional Guidance Scale.* Lola Jones offers something similar called an *Instrument Panel.*

These scales are a great gage to identify vibrational frequencies. High vibrational frequencies are love, ecstasy, enlightenment, freedom and empowerment to name a few. Lower vibrational frequencies are linked to feelings like fear, rage, revenge, shame, frustration and blame. The goal is to be a vibrational match to whatever you desire from the Universe.

Trust My Feelings?

It's absolutely important to trust your feelings. But even more important is to *feel your feelings.* When you understand the significance of your feelings and their divine intention, you'll recognize them as being instrumental in producing happiness.

This might seem frightening as feelings make some of us uncomfortable.

For me, feelings have been the place of my deepest self-discovery. I used to think that if I felt my feelings, I would be overwhelmed by them. Allowing myself to be vulnerable felt like being exposed. The fear of being vulnerable is rooted in a fear of being seen for who we are (which is what we really want).

Going a level deeper, the true fear is being judged. Over the years I've learned how to recognize someone who is safe to be vulnerable with. I also know when I'm in a space where I can be open and authentic. These are places I can share my deepest truths. Putting words to those feelings is an even deeper journey of self-discovery.

We are all in this together. Sometimes we stand in front of the mirror and critique ourselves about what isn't the way we think it should be.

We struggle to fit in. We feel alone, unseen, invisible and even unworthy. We might struggle to trust ourselves because of what we think of as past mistakes. Trusting our heart might've gotten us hurt. We use these experiences and outcomes as the gage for future decisions.

Picture for a moment a river where skillful beavers have built a dam. That's how it is when our emotions aren't felt, expressed or honored. Those damned-up emotions can keep your vibrational frequency at a low number.

You say you don't have time to feel your feelings. But ask yourself this, do you have time to keep struggling, stressing, and denying yourself peace and confidence with money? If you are ready to move forward with *Money Mastery Now*, be sure to download your personal *Diving into Feelings* audio link in the Resource section.

Slow down for a minute and think about the money choices you are making. What are the feelings behind your most recent purchases? How often do you allow your unconscious feelings to govern your choices and actions with money? From clothing to vacations to real estate–what do you feel when you are spending? This is a good starting place for your journey to financial wellness.

The Value of You

In 2015, in the midst of a meditation session, I heard my inner being clearly say, "Choose you. Love who you are, not just what you do." Then I heard the voice of the Dalai Lama. The message I heard was, "It will be the Western woman who will change the world. My first thought was "Change the world? We can barely change ourselves. How will we change the world?"

I typed the message I heard into the computer. To my surprise, I got a powerful confirmation. There was a recording of The Dalai Lama saying, "The world will be saved by the western woman."

This talk was delivered during the *Vancouver Peace Summit* in 2009. It opened on Sunday morning, September 27, 2009.

Here I was in 2015, six years later, hearing this drop into my spirit. I thought this topic could be my next book as well as a powerful platform to empower women. This message encouraged women to choose themselves over slaving, working hard, ignoring their health, their needs and personal desires. His message is and was an invitation for women to step up and that we have the power to make an impact and influence the course of history.

I took that as a call to all women, myself included, to love who we *are* and NOT just what we do.

Loving who we are seems like a simple task. But many women struggle with loving themselves. Women choose instead to take on role after role, some fulfilling and some not so much, under the premise that what we *do* is valuable. It's time for women to ask themselves, "What would I *be* if I wasn't *doing*?" This was the very question I asked myself in 2015 after visiting a friend I hadn't seen since college. He prepared dinner for us. When I finished my dinner and stood up with my plate he said, "Put your plate down." I thought to myself, "You're not the boss of me." I proceeded to take a step toward taking my plate to the sink.

Again, I heard, "Put your plate down." This time the tone of the second request was gentle but firm. I sat down and put my plate on the table. I thought maybe he wanted to say something to me. After a few seconds, I realized he was watching television and enjoying the rest of his meal. I got up again, left my plate on the table and went into the living room to sit on the couch. As soon as I sat down, I felt tightness in my throat and began coughing.

I felt a puddle of water building up in my eyes that soon trickled down my cheeks.

I silently asked myself, "Who am I if I'm not doing?"

There was an emptiness within as the question bounced off the walls of my being. At the time, I didn't know the answer. I had never asked myself that question before.

Many of us struggle to separate what we do from who we are. It was my first coach, Lisa Nichols, who demonstrated what it meant to give from my overflow (my saucer) rather than my cup, so to speak. After that demonstration, I realized that in all my doing and doing, I was empty. I had placed my entire sense of value

and worth on what I was doing.
Since my meditation in 2015
I learned that my value is grounded
in my essence, my unique beingness.

This wisdom keeps me from
shrinking based on what others do or
don't do. We must shift our focus
from doing for others, to BEING and
KNOWING our value.

Spending Habits and Addiction

With the increase of online shopping
on Amazon, QVC and other channels,
our spending habits show that we are
compulsive shopaholics, (emotional
shopping) and trophy shopaholics
always shopping for the perfect item.
We are also bargain shoppers
(chasing a sale), collectors (needing
one thing in every color) and bulimic
shoppers. Many women are
unknowingly addicted to the
feelings, the euphoric rush and the

anxiety of shopping. Think about how many times you and/or you and friends go for what's called retail therapy. Just the fact that our shopping has a title says it all!

We are all aware of friends or it might be you, who shop and hide the items they purchased in their closet. Why do we hide these items? Usually, it's because they weren't in our budget.

Maybe it's because we're violating an agreement with ourselves or our husband/wife/partner. More importantly, what drives us to make the purchase when we know we have financial goals. We made a commitment to debt elimination, a great vacation, real estate investments, other investing, college tuition or retirement? What's the trigger that makes us throw caution to the wind and tell ourselves we'll deal with the bill when it comes.

We made a choice to further enslave ourselves in the Money Loop. We say we want to get out of the Money Loop. We're stressed, tired of worrying and want something different for our life. Underneath these actions is a story of unaddressed value and sense of worth. What shows up time and time again with people that I coach is an unwillingness to face underlying pain and dissatisfaction. Whether you're an entrepreneur who doesn't charge for the value you offer your clients or the single woman shopping for an outfit who already has tagged dresses in her closet. You have to get in touch with the underlying issues behind your overspending. In becoming conscious spenders, we must acknowledge our habits and how we betray our goals and our

hearts by not honoring our financial
commitments.

Sexual Transmutation

After reading the book *Think and Grow Rich* for the umpteenth time, I found myself drawn to the chapter on Sexual Transmutation.

Think and Grow Rich author, Napoleon Hill, says, "Sex, love and faith are the most powerful emotions because of their ability to impact our thinking and influence us to achieve what we may have before thought impossible."

Hill is correct. Sex, love and faith are three energies that dwell within each of us. When activated, these energies can influence us to achieve what at one point we thought was impossible. I read this book every year. And every year I understood that powerful nugget more deeply. Sexual transmutation was the lesson this year.

Sexual experience can be many things to many people. One of those things is pleasure and intense energy. Sexual transmutation is our ability to take these powerful energies of sexuality, eroticism and femininity and use them as fuel to achieve our hearts desire. Think of how you've procrastinated on your dream project such as writing a book, poetry, love letter or proposal. Imagine being in a sensual energy or being fully in your feminine presence such that you can feel energy vibrating and flowing through your body. Instead of doing what you've normally done with this energy you intentionally focus it on taking inspired actions for your goals. You take the pen in hand, grab your journal and begin to write or outline your ideas. You write out a plan of action to complete the project. This is what I did after reading the chapter on Sex Transmutation in Think and Grow Rich.

I became intentional about being present to my energy and focused it on completing a product that I had been pushing around on my desk.

Sex. Trauma. Money.

During the above-mentioned reading I pondered how many women have been touched by trauma that shut down their feelings of being fully in their bodies. The trauma of being violated impacts our relationship with ourselves and unconsciously with our money too.

Secrets eat away at our heart and blocking our money flow. For several years I hosted a, "Sex, Money & Trauma," online support call that attracted women from all ages and walks of life. The call was an invitation to participate in a private conversation about the impact of trauma, specifically violations, on our heart as well as our relationship with money. Women (and men too) live with so many hurts, betrayals and violations that we have not shared with anyone. How do we show up in our relationship with money when we carry scars from unaddressed violations? The women I mentor in my Real Money Matters group have shared a pattern of engaging in unplanned spending.

One woman said on the call, "You buy things you don't need and don't use."

This is just the beginning of how unhealed trauma shows up in our relationship with money. Buying items, we don't need and ultimately don't use is one-way trauma shows up. The deeper wounds show up as unconscious shopping.

Every time we betray a money goal (be it a savings fund, family vacation, college savings, etc.), we chip away at our self-esteem and money confidence.

To help us determine whether unhealed trauma is spearheading our spending habits, we must review our purchases over a three-month period. Specifically, write down or log the items you purchase with a focus on impulsive, unconscious purchases. Total the actual cost of unconscious purchases at the end of each day. Then do it weekly and lastly, for the entire month. What's your total?

Releasing Your Hurts

Most of us were taught to forgive and forget the hurts we've suffered in our life. This premise was based on the golden rule, "Do unto others as you would have them do unto you." I'll forgive you and you'll forgive me, or you will forgive me because I forgive you.

It makes sense. However, this theory runs into a glitch when the other person either doesn't forgive.

You were disappointed, hurt and betrayed. It's hard to think of forgiving the person who hurt you, not to mention letting it be forgotten. I remember those times. In hindsight, my dear friends were really patient with me. Many of my calls came from a place of being a victim disguised as hurt and feeling like poor me. When your heart is broken, it can be hard to take responsibility for your part in the scenario.

You hold the scenario close. You promise yourself it won't happen again because you won't let it. You work hard to never let your guard down in hopes of not experiencing that pain again.

This is a powerful scenario many are familiar with.

Forgiveness is about being willing to give ourselves second and third chances to be happy, fulfilled and in alignment with our goals and dreams.

One of the first workshops I facilitated was on, "Forgiveness: How to Forgive *and* Forget." The common thought held by most people in attendance was, "I'll forgive but I won't forget."

Is this your perception on forgiveness?

Let's look at this idea of forgiving but not forgetting. Not forgetting the injury supports our avoidance of recognizing the poor choices we've made in relationships, health and financially.
I knew first-hand the reasons why I shouldn't forget. If I didn't forget, I thought it wouldn't happen again. If I didn't forget, I'd make a better choice next time.

But the glue that holds the decision not to forget is the very feelings of hurt, anger, betrayal and disappointment. Unless we release these feelings we really aren't forgiving. This isn't so much about letting go of our feelings about the person who harmed us. It's about recognizing our feelings about ourselves.

The more we stand guard protecting our heart, the longer we hold the offender hostage, the more likely we are to imprison ourselves along with them. We are in danger of handcuffing ourselves to our past trauma.

We tell ourselves that forgetting the offense means letting the offending person off the hook. We keep them tethered by continuing to blame them. As time goes on, we make them responsible for all our feelings of anger, sadness and fear.

What we don't realize is we're the ones holding the handle of the hook. Letting go of the blame and the anger sets us free to heal, learn the lesson and empower ourselves.

Forgiveness Never Was About Them

Forgiveness isn't about him, her, them or it. Forgiveness is about YOU.

It's about unhooking yourself from the story that you keep repeating, feeding and retelling. It's about you looking within and finding the nugget of wisdom from the experience, keeping it for the future and letting the experience itself go. It was never about milking the experience for days and years or wearing it as a badge of honor. Nor is it about singing the "somebody done me wrong," song forever.

Some of us have this notion that everything here on earth is supposed to be comfortable. Or maybe because of being born into a physical body we thought life would feel like the womb. In the instances when life doesn't feel good, we label it as bad or painful.

The times that make us feel good are labeled good and happy. How much time do we spend trying to avoid pain at the expense of our own happiness?

Each experience we attract is designed to teach us something about ourselves. While we prefer to feel comfortable, it's rare to experience the fire of alchemy--which is necessary for our personal transformation--alongside happiness. It's while walking through and living with the choices we make that we discover the deepest treasures of ourselves. In each experience, we have the opportunity to practice our life skills. We also learn lessons about yin and yang, stillness, patience, compassion, setting boundaries, self-love and much more.

Radical Forgiveness

At one point in my life, I was in the process of ending a long-term relationship, releasing my spiritual community and embracing a present. That present was my beautiful chocolate drop of a Precious son. All of these major events moved me into a deep period of personal transformation. I remember feeling so unsure of myself in the midst of actually being sure. I felt so alone without my mother or grandmother's strength to draw upon.

One evening I remember not being able to catch my breath because I was crying so hard. I just couldn't seem to see clearly enough to comprehend everything that was happening in my experience. Feelings of betrayal coursed through my veins. Self-doubt was rampant. My self-worth was hard to hold on to given my personal judgments and internal attacks. I had unknowingly been carrying this experience as a badge of honor. "Look what happened to me. It's not fair."

That wasn't getting me anywhere. After many months into it, after attending a silent spiritual retreat, I began to gain some of my power back. I remember standing in my kitchen looking out the window in somewhat of a trance. In that moment, I decided I was done. I could no longer live in a place of feeling like a victim.

Several days later that I stumbled upon the book *Radical Forgiveness* by Colin Tipping and its accompanying transformative forgiveness worksheet. (See Resources.) Forgiveness was presented in a way that allowed me to claim my pain and justifications, while stepping into healing my heart and moving into alignment.

This process is effective if you follow it. Specifically, the Radical Forgiveness worksheet is what allowed me to experience healing, regain a sense of power and a gradual sense of resolve. Don't get me wrong, it's not easy. You may have to complete the worksheet several times.

Through the radical forgiveness process and choosing to be radically honest each time you complete a worksheet, you'll free the space in your heart. You'll also elevate your energy and your vibrational frequency. That alignment ultimately aligns you with money energy. Releasing old hurts is the equivalent of unclogging a drain. Think of that swishing sound the water makes as it flows down a cleared drain. This is what awaits you in releasing your hurts.

What's Your Come From

When I speak about your "come from," I'm attempting to capture the energy that is driving you. Motive is also a good word for this.

Are you coming from a consciousness of abundance and infinite possibilities? Or is your "come from" a place of prosperity and wealth consciousness? The energy of these thoughts vibrates at a high frequency that matches winning the lottery, having access to unlimited money and wealth. On the other hand, if your desire to win the lottery is rooted in scarcity, desperation, fear or worry, the energy would vibrate at a very low frequency. That doesn't match the vibrational frequency needed to win a large sum of money. Thus your, "come from," is scarcity and lack.

Think of it this way, you're looking for Cool Jazz on a Classical or Country channel. They don't match.

Money is Light

If I haven't made it clear let me say that money is a high, light vibration. The only thing that weighs money down is us with our thoughts and inherited beliefs about it. On its own money is simply an outward expression of an internal vibrational frequency that is supported by a powerfully trained mind and an aligned mindset.

Money doesn't walk, talk, move or anything else. It doesn't even have the power to be evil or burn a hole in your pocket. It can't be spent on its own. It has nothing to do with us not being good with money. It doesn't think of itself as a limited resource. It doesn't care if you work hard or smart for it or if you think it's selfish to want more of it. It doesn't think it makes you happy or sad, unless you say so.

Money is an inanimate object…period. We are the ones that make money heavy with all of our hang ups, outdated beliefs, frustrations and unconscious actions. These are some of the thoughts that many of you have in your relationship with money. If these were the thoughts your current lover, partner, spouse or BFF had about you would you feel aligned with them?

Embrace the principle that everything is made of energy and that everything is connected. At the core of existence, you and money are made of the same substance. It's just that money's energy is paper while our energy is as physical human beings.

This is no different than the energy you feel between you and someone you are physically and sexually attracted to. You can communicate with the person you're attracted to from across the room and never open your mouth. How? By sending energy through your gestures, movements, eyes, lips and posture.

The invisible aspect of money is attracted to the aligned, high-vibing, invisible aspect of you.

TAKE ACTION

Reflect on the suggestions, questions and statements below to strengthen your ability to make responsible spending choices:

1. Track your feelings

2. Track the words you say to yourself at the time of a purchase.

3. Are you convincing yourself to spend?

4. What do you feel in that moment?

5. Do you have a budget?

6. Is this purchase part of your budget?

7. What do you tell yourself to make it acceptable to forfeit your goals?

8. What makes it okay for you not to honor your feelings by spending?

Practice Forgiveness

Ho'oponopono is considered a prayer or a mantra with the intention of forgiveness and reconciliation. I was introduced to Ho'oponopono through my studies with Dr. Joe Vitale. There are four powerful phrases in this mantra:

1. I love you.

2. I'm sorry.

3. Please forgive me.

4. Thank-you.

The goal is to say these statements when feelings of anger, disappointment or betrayal rise up. Say the prayer once for yourself, once for the person you want to forgive and once to God.

Do note, sometimes professional support may be needed to overcome and heal severe trauma.

Chapter Five-Align Your Inspired Action – Frustrated or Frazzled

The highest most powerful action you can take is inspired action.

Jenenne Macklin

What is it that keeps you feeling frustrated and frazzled in your relationship with money?

I was very good at taking frazzled action motivated by fear or worry. Usually it was because an unexpected bill was due or because my spending and earning numbers didn't match. From the outside looking in, it was easy to see that my money

management skills were the trigger.
I didn't have all the savvy
information about budgeting, but I
did have basic math skills to add and
subtract. What I had to learn was
how to consistently take inspired
action.

Inspired Action

Before we look at what inspired
action is, ask yourself, when was the
last time you said, "I should have
followed my first mind?" What
wisdom was being shared with you
in that moment? Why didn't you
trust it? Taking inspired action is the
ultimate goal in aligning your
relationship with money.

Taking inspired action calls you to
recognize your power within.
Inspired action positions you to
receive the fulfillment you desire.
These actions keep you in the flow of

creating AND achieving your goals.
You possess the power to take
incremental internal actions using
your thoughts, words and feelings.
This process will help you create the
life you desire and deserve.

Thoughts, words, feelings and
inspired action are dynamic energies
which vibrate at frequencies that
communicate to the Universe. These
vibrations attract matching
frequencies that produce results in
our life.

When we're aligned and intentional,
we can create powerful thoughts.
We can also daydream in color and
possibilities. The same is true for our
words. When we're aligned in our
spoken word, we can speak our
dreams, aspirations and purpose into
reality. Our feelings are the fuel that
powers our thoughts, words and
intentions.

Thoughts and words are significant because they are the foundation for our actions. Not just any action, but inspired action because that brings the highest possibility of achieving our goals.

The main questions to consider in our taking inspired action is, "What actions do I take?" and "When do I take them?"

Many of you find gratification in being in action because it feels like you're accomplishing something. However, unplanned, frantic, frazzled action usually wastes time, energy and money. If you are an entrepreneur or a small business owner, frazzled service can cost you time, money, clients and possibly even partnerships.

Taming the desire to act without a clear strategy or plan requires discipline, at least in the beginning. Some of us suffer from the busy body syndrome which keeps us in perpetual motion. Once we understand the value of having a strategy or plan, we're more willing, if not insistent, on engaging in a process that ignites "inspired action."

Action Is Action, Right?

Yes, action is action. But we're not just talking about any kind of action. Not at all. We're talking about "inspired" action. What's the difference? The key word is inspired.

Think of the last time you were inspired. Was that a high energy or what? Close your eyes and reminisce for a moment on the feeling of being inspired. Powerful, right? Goosebumps? Heart activated and flowing…yes? Were you fully engrossed in the experience? That's the energy you're tapping into when you take inspired action.

Was it an inspirational talk you listened to? A movie you were watching? Whatever it was, start to capture for yourself just what triggers your feeling of being inspired. Become familiar with how this energy feels.

On the other hand, also become conscious of your day-to-day actions and their energy. Are they often hurried, rushed or impulsive? Are you on automatic pilot, moving through your day just trying to get things done?
If you're anything like I was, you are simply checking things off your to-do list.

Tell me if any of these seem familiar: stopping at Starbucks for your morning fix or shot of Frappuccino. Rushing to your office, train station or congested freeway. Rushing to meet deadlines while at work or in your business to meet quarter earning goals. Going home, stopping by the gym (oops had to take that off the list), cooking dinner, writing your blog. Paying bills online, falling into bed later than your body requires. Feeling dead tired only to get up and do it all over again. This is the model so many of us have inherited from our mothers, fathers, family and friends. You will be happy to know that one hour of inspired action can replace hours of busybody, got-to-get-it-done-so -I-feel-like-I'm-doing-something energy.

Reflect again on the feeling of being inspired. I was just watching a movie called *Million Dollar Arm* and I felt inspired by the journey of the two young boys that were brought to the United States to play baseball. Each moment that I felt inspired, my heartbeat was accompanied by goosebumps popping up all over my arms and body. That's the way it felt for me.

Now it's your turn. Think back to a time you felt inspired. How did the energy feel? Where were you when inspiration showed up. What does your mind do or not do when you are inspired?

Inspired action is fun, light flowing energy.

Inspired action guides us to our dreams. It's heart-stirring and elevating. It has the power to silence the mind.

Inspired action feels like our dreams and goals calling us. We feel the stirring within as we are called to create, express, share and manifest. When you've been ignited by inspiration and passion it's a yummy feeling, right?

Sometimes I still have to remind myself to work from inspired action rather than anxious energy that tells me to do something just to do it.

Your inspired action experience will happen in many different ways. One of the ways I notice my inspired action is with cooking. I have no problem creating a new meal from scratch several times during the week. This is purely an inspired action.

From the moment I hear myself say, "I want to cook chicken a different way," I get ideas for different ingredients to use for a rub. I think about whether to use balsamic, wild or brown rice or include soups and other spices. I am guided toward what to use and the entire process is anchored from within i.e. internal actions for external results.

Pull out your journal and capture your own inspired actions. Write

about times you wrote a powerful
spoken word piece, made that
uncomfortable phone call. Maybe
you designed a fierce hairstyle or
dress for a client, completely
redecorated your bedroom, created a
beautiful cake that everyone loved,
wrote a love letter to yourself or
offered a powerful, soul-stirring
apology.

One of my larger inspired actions
was to run a marathon at the age of
50.

I was inspired to run a marathon by
Oprah Winfrey who was also
running a marathon. I sat with the
thought and waited for the feeling of
it to show up. The excitement was
ignited when I went to the first
training session. Do you know how
long I had to train to run the
marathon? It took nine months of
training because I injured myself

during my second weekend of
training.

I began training in the Fall before my
50th birthday and continued into the
Spring of the following year. I live in
California. In California, we typically
have great weather year-round. But
during my marathon training, I had
my fair share of hot days, cold days,
warm and rainy days. While I did
have help from time to time, I often
ran by myself anywhere from five to
twenty miles.

We were given a running schedule
for our weekly runs.

On the weekends, I ran with my
running team, the LA Roadrunners at
Santa Monica Beach.

On the actual day of my race I had
even more tangible and much needed
support. First of all, it was a perfect

day, at the start of the race. The temperature in Los Angeles was approximately 60°F. Halfway through the race it started to drizzle. It was cute at first. By mile 18 it was no longer cute, and I just wanted it to be over.

While I hadn't anticipated anything but running and keeping a decent pace so that the truck wouldn't sweep me up at the end for being the last runner, several of my friends who were runners had anticipated that I would need support. They decided to come and run the balance of the race with me at mile 20. What a blast of energy that was!

Without their help I'm sure I would have decided to walk. Soaking wet, in running shorts, a tank top, and totally exhausted, my friends ran with me to the entry gates releasing me to run across the finish line to complete the race.

During this process, I discovered a secret ingredient to inspired action. This energy is so very powerful that it can sustain us for the duration of a project or until the manifestation of our dreams.

As fun, flowing and powerful as inspired action is, it is dependent upon us being open to follow the energy where it leads us. It's dependent on us listening to and trusting it's guidance by taking the prescribed action it offers.

The movie, *The Secret,* convinced many people there was minimal effort needed to align with the universal Law of Attraction. This could not be further from the truth.

Sitting and waiting for inspiration to show up while we do nothing does not connect us to the Law of Attraction. Aligning our energy with what we desire to attract is our primary contribution to the process.

The Universe is waiting on us to give it our orders, to take aligned action and be open and ready to receive. Nowhere in the process of inspired action is there an invitation to sit and wait.

That song we like that tingles our heart and soul was probably created at 3 o'clock in the morning by inspired action. The speaker who stood up and told the story that empowered you, the composer, author, runner, cyclist...all of them are acting from inspired action.

You already know about inspired action and have experienced it

through the still small voice
whispering in your heart or ear.
Inspired action is the nudge from the
Universe that usually frighten us as
it beckons us to change our behavior.
It also calls us to show up, write that
book, set a boundary with our
money, schedule an appointment
with the doctor for that recurring
pain or even to leave a relationship.

The Universe is always trying to get
us to take inspired action toward
what we say we desire. It's a built-in
partnership with our success. When
we aren't aware of this partnership,
we ignore its wisdom. What other
reason would there be to ignore the
divine inspiration being ignited
within?

We don't trust it.

We don't think the Universe will
support us? Or is it because inspired

action calls us to be more authentic
in our living?

Inspired action will touch and
transform our heart and expose us to
a higher energetic version of
ourselves. In other words, inspired
action requires us to be mildly to
moderately uncomfortable.

What also causes us to ignore it, is
our perception of how we should
hear the information. The voice
within sounds just like our own
voice, only a heck of a lot smarter.
Although sometimes it may be a
voice within, other times it may be a
feeling of everything falling into
place.

What each of us gets to do, to one
degree or another, is to listen, trust
and follow its guidance. The
Universe is communicating to you.

Inspired action is the highest energy possible to fuel our efforts and will easily transmit the most aligned vibration that produces the best results. The key to taking inspired action is to recognize that action comes from within. That action may excite and frighten us at the same time.

PRACTICE

Set aside a day to tune into inspired action. When you wake up, tell the Universe you are open to taking inspired action in your business, at your place of employment or with your health. Listen as you go through day. Notice what you feel and what stirs your heart. As you listen and feel, just begin to take notice of how the inspiration feels. Understand that in the beginning, your inspired action may be to call or

visit someone or write notes about a
project.

Whatever it is, for this dedicated
period of time simply BE willing to
notice how it feels for you to be
inspired from within.

On other occasions, direct yourself to
be aware of nudges you hear or feel
and commit to following its
guidance. Write these in your
journal so that you can see just how
many times you are stirred by the
Universe.

Following this guidance as your way
of saying yes to the call and letting
the Universe know you're paying
attention. Whether it is a whisper to
make a specific phone call, turn
down a particular street, call the
book editor, sign-up for a class, I urge
you to follow the guidance. Think of
it as a game. In the beginning each

nudge is the Universe checking to see if you're paying attention and if you will follow the guidance.

Think of this as a relationship like any other relationship that starts slow, you get acquainted and then blossom into a full partnership. This will strengthen your ability to receive your personal divine wisdom.

Believe Something New

What would it take for you to think something different or consider something new?

According to experts, we have approximately 80,000 thoughts each day. That's an average of 3,300 thoughts per hour. There are quite a few thoughts going through our minds. When I began to pay attention to my thoughts, the most interesting thing was how many were repetitive. Some were even full conversations with different variations of the same thought.

I remember thinking this work was a total waste of energy. I thought it was the equivalent of watching a dog chase its tail around and around. I realized that the vibrational frequency of this type of unconscious creating wasn't high enough to move me toward my goals.

As I looked a little deeper, I realize some of these thoughts were outdated scenarios and beliefs. How could I just continue to think the same thoughts over and over? I was being unconscious at the helm and going through my days on autopilot. At the time though it seemed like the most efficient way to get everything done.

I began to pay attention to what I was thinking. At first, I wrote down my daily thoughts as a way to reprogram myself. Repetition had worked for my son when he was learning his ABC's.

I thought maybe it could work for me as a way to learn a new way of thinking. I began to think of my mind as a computer that would think what I trained it to think. I would repeat certain thoughts while standing in the mirror. I wrote the thoughts out five times each on 3x5 index cards.

These were some of those thoughts:

- *I live in infinite possibilities every day.*

- *There is more than enough to go around.*

- *I am a one of a kind divine design.*

- *I am focusing within today.*

- *I am divinely guided.*

- *I am capable and fully equipped to
create a prosperous life.*

- *I trust and know that there is more
than enough to go around.*

The way that I began to believe
something new was one step at a
time. Think about it, that's how we
have learned so much of what we
know – writing it down and then
repeating it. From the alphabet to
speeches, to presentations, it's been
with one thought at a time.

I've always been a doodler, so I would
write out a new thought to think
then post it on a 3x5 card next to my

bed and on my bathroom mirror to read each morning and evening.

You have the power to think whatever you choose, so why not be conscious about creating a bigger version of yourself, your life and your possibilities?

Trusting What You Hear

At the beginning of this chapter I asked when the last time was you remember saying, "I should have followed my first mind?" If not that specific phrase, maybe you said, "I just knew...," or "Something told me..."

Your reference was that you heard a soft whisper and decided (this is your power in action) to discount, ignore or question its validity? Several hours, days or weeks later when truth showed up with laser sharp accuracy, you said, "I should have followed my first mind."

Reflect on this statement and get your journal out to record your answer. "The reason I don't listen, trust or follow the still small voice I hear is because…"

I hosted a call on the topic of intuition at one of my first coaching programs. During the call, I asked one of my callers "Who do you think is speaking to you? Her response was, "I know it's God, Rev., but I don't have time." All I could do was smile.

What could we be missing out on because we don't listen to or take action on the divine guidance of the still small voice?

From a very young age I was
encouraged to listen to and trust the
still small voice that I heard. My
parents separated and I lived with
my mother. When I was about
twelve years old, my mom went on a
date. Afterwards she and her date
stopped at a taco stand up the street
from our home. As I prepared for
bed, I heard a crash. The silence was
pierced by the sound of a single
hubcap rolling down the street. In an
instant, something propelled me
forward.

I grabbed my robe, slipping my right
arm in and then my left while
reaching for the knob to our front
door. I nearly stumbled down the
three steps to the walkway. I turned
right and screamed at the top of my
lungs, "*Momma! Momma! Momma!*"
as I ran down the street to the corner
intersection.

I arrived at the corner to discover my mother had been in a car accident, rear-ended while parked.

What happened? What was the force that propelled me out the door? What was it about the hubcap that triggered the alarm within me? Later my mother would ask me how I knew something had happened to her. I told her I just knew. Her response remains with me to this day. She simply said, "You always know. Remember that."

In spite of that magical moment with my inner guidance, honoring the voice within wasn't an immediate practice. As I got older, I expanded and included using my intuition and my first mind as tools for living life.

I grew to cherish and respect the whispers no matter how much they frightened me. It took time for me to live as I do now--listening to the small still voice within. Today I depend on it for guidance, insight, individualized coaching strategies, speaking topics, Facebook posts and understanding personal dynamics with others. For me, it doesn't get any better than having direct divine guidance.

We don't have to call our girlfriends, boyfriend, mother, father or anyone else. We can always get a direct download of information, wisdom and directives.

Take it from best-selling author and entrepreneur, Joe Vitale. In the movie, The *Secret*, he says, "The Universe likes speed. Don't delay. Don't second guess. Don't doubt. When the opportunity is there, when the impulse is there, when the intuitive nudge from within is there,

act. That's your job. And that's all
you have to do."

There is universal law that
encourages us to heed our intuitive
nudge from within as our guide for
when to take inspired action.

Trusting what we hear within is a
powerful action. We should give
ourselves room to experience this
fully. Practice hearing the hunches,
nudges or any other divine
communication of Spirit. Use these
three steps to begin.

PRACTICE

1. For the next week, pick several
    days that you agree not to ask for
    advice outside of yourself. Decide
    that you will only listen for the
    still small voice within. Simply

whisper to your Higher self in
your morning ritual that you are
listening today.

2. Make a commitment to write
    down what you hear. No matter
    what happens just write it down.

3. If you choose to act on what you
    hear, or if you hesitate or ignore it,
    completely write that down too.

4. In those instances where you take
    action, write in your journal your
    experience. In those cases where
    you don't take the directed action,
    write what your inner struggle
    and conversation to yourself was.

5. What made you not follow the
    direct guidance? This is all done
    from a place of observation only.
    No judgment.

6. Wait a few days and pick another week to notice just how much the Universe is really communicating with you. You may have been too busy, distracted or simply ignoring it before or maybe you don't trust it.

Think of what's been waiting to be heard and trusted by you all this time. Recognize that you are receiving up-to-the-minute, first-hand information and divine wisdom from Source. From where I stand, it doesn't get any better than that.

Accessing the Within

One of the stories I read many years ago and never forgot refers to an ancient truth. It confirms what many spiritual teachers, gurus, shamans and philosophers have shared which is, "Within us are infinitely rare and magnificent treasures that are innate: worth, value, joy, wisdom, love."

There is an Eastern tale about how at one-point humanity consisted of all gods. We lost our power after misusing it. Brahma, the head God in the Hindu tradition, met with the other Gods to discuss where to place the power humanity had misused. The Gods considered relocating to the ocean but knew man would go to the depth of the oceans to find them. They considered the highest mountain but again knew that man would scale that too.

So, in the end, the Gods decided to place themselves in the one place man would never think to look: *within himself.* And as the story goes, since that time, man has been looking everywhere for a treasure that lies within.

Access to the within happens when we're willing to accept there is a power beating our heart. That same power is breathing our breath for us every moment without judgement, penalty, exchange or debt. Not to mention the simple fact that we didn't create ourselves. From the moment the spark of life was breathed into our being, we've been inseparable from the Presence that gives us life. That presence is called by many names: God, Spirit, Shiva, Jesus, Brahma, Allah, Krishna, Vishnu, Buddha, Large Self, Source, Goddess and Olodumare, to name a few.

What does it take to expand our self-identification and self-perception to honor this Divine Oneness? What would help our heart know, beyond a shadow of a doubt, that there is an invisible, divine, spiritual aspect to us? That aspect is irrevocably connected to an omnipotent, omnipresent, omniscient energy that represents all life.

What practice is likely to cause a significant impact on our energetic vibration, as well as our sense of purpose and partnership with the Source? Jot down your reflections and answers to these questions in your journal.

You've probably heard and maybe even attempted the practice of meditation. Meditation is a fundamental practice for continued growth in clarity, self-worth, inner peace and the calm in the storm.

Studies have shown that increased concentration, more restful sleep, increased self-confidence and creativity are just a few benefits of meditation. As a tool for alignment, take time to sit in stillness for fifteen minutes each morning and evening. This practice will help position you for greater success.

No matter what you've heard about meditation or even if you've attempted it once, meditation is doable. You may have to sit on a pillow on the floor or in a chair or on the bed. You might have to start with guided meditation first (see the Resources section). Either way, you must begin preparing your body temple for the money and prosperity you desire. Training your mind and disciplining your body to work for you can produce the perfect balance.

I found myself on a spiritual quest
for a deeper understanding.

I initially taught myself to meditate
from reading books. Then some
years later I joined Siddha Yoga
Meditation and deepened my practice
under the guidance of Gurumayi
Chidvilasananda.

My monkey mind and its distractive
tendency made it difficult to master
mediation. But once I learned to
witness the thoughts rather than
engage with them or give them
attention, I gradually begin to find
my way into deeper stillness. I know
the same can be true for you.

The more we're able to intentionally
BE in the stillness, the better the
seeds of our dreams can take root and
evolve. Withdrawing from the
external world of noise into the
silence anchors our soul. When we

can BE in the oneness, the greater us
can fully mature.

PRACTICE

Write a promise and a declaration to
one of your goals. State your
commitment to being the container
for the goal to grow.

For example:

I, (insert your name), accept that
what I desire and deserve is within
reach.
I recognize myself as the vehicle
from which my goal will manifest.
Today (insert the date) I commit and
declare that I will tend to the garden
of my mind removing any weeds of
fear or doubt by establishing and
following a meditative practice.

257

Name:

Date:

Witness:

If possible, have someone witness your declaration. It's good to have someone hold you accountable to the goals, dreams and accomplishments you desire in your life.

Post your declaration somewhere in your home so that you can read it out loud each morning.

Give your practice a name such as: Intention Setting. Practicing the Presence. Being in Stillness. Honoring My Dreams.

Find a comfortable spot to sit where you won't be disturbed. Focus on your breathing while you sit in silence. Focusing on your breathing means you notice your inhale and then your exhale. As you focus on your breathing, notice if your breathing is shallow or is your breathing slow and easy? Try to count how long it takes to complete the inhale.

What number do you get to?

Likewise, when you count your exhale how long does it take?

As you focus your attention and awareness on breathing, your breathing will deepen. As you give your attention to your breathing, it will slowly align.

We naturally have equal exhales and inhales. Feel your breathing expand and deepen as you get into the rhythm.

After each session, take time to make notes about your breathing, how you felt during the session, how still you became inside. Monitor how you feel during the remainder of the day.

Allow this to become a practice that you use throughout the day to come back to center when annoyed, frustrated or overwhelmed.

Power of Forgiveness

In Chapter 3, we explored concepts of forgiveness. We learned that forgiveness isn't about who we're holding anger, a grudge or disappointment with. Forgiveness is for and about us and our happiness. Forgiveness is about healing our heart. Forgiveness is a path to being and living in alignment with our goals and dreams.

This chapter of *Money Mastery Now* brings us back to the door of forgiveness. We explore forgiveness as an inspired action with proven results. Forgiveness should be a go-to practice to shift energy and elevate our vibrational frequency.

This step requires consistent completion of the Radical Forgiveness sheet to keep our energy

high and aligned for maximum
results.

Rather than feeling frustration, we
take comfort in completing our
worksheets. We contemplate what
our experience has come to teach us.
We evaluate how long we've
harbored feelings about it.

Every time we return to the hurt,
anger or disappointment from a
previous offense, we recognize that it
blocks our progress. We can't align if
we're in hurt and anger. Instead of
immersing ourselves into the old
pain, I encourage readers to grab
another worksheet and release the
hurt. This will create an internal
shift for you to move back into
alignment with the results you
desire.

This process is about aligning with a
vibrational frequency that matches

the vibration of our dreams and goals. This is one of the practices we can use to keep the space clear where we connect with our larger goals.

Remember, there is no such thing as hiding our feelings. Just because we don't talk about or share them won't make them go away. Our feelings are energy. The goal for aligning and creating is to live in a state of high energy at least 75% of the time. Forgiving is a heart and soul releasing experience. Letting go of what no longer serves us is all that we are doing. It no longer serves us to hate, cry, complain, hold onto or judge ourselves and others. It no longer serves our goals and dreams to give energy to the past or allow anger, disappointment, betrayal or fear to deprive us of our prosperous life. That's what not forgiving does—it clogs our energy field and slows down our results.

PRACTICE

Get in the habit of asking yourself,
"Who or what do I need to forgive
today?"

Once we identify the story that we've
been nursing and allowing to zap our
energy, it's time to begin the process
of releasing so we can receive. When
we've been hurt deeply or it's been
pushed down for so long, we may
need to use the Radical Forgiveness
Worksheet to raise our vibration.
(See the Resources section)

The Power of Your Attention

In *Money Mastery Now* we learn about
the energies in the world that desire
our attention. From targeted
television commercials to skillfully
marketed advertisements to bosses,
employers and employees. From our
parents to our young and adult

children--our attention to others is
significant. When we understand
the power of where we place our
attention, we see clearly the path to
align us with the external results we
desire.

Would we rather spend all day
putting our attention on something
that makes us sick, gives us a
headache, makes our stomach upset
or fills us with anxiety? Or would we
choose to place our attention on what
keeps our vibrational frequency high
and keeps us on track for achieving
our results?

The energy on which we direct our
attention is incredibly powerful.
What we consistently focus our
attention on is what we allow into
our vibration and life. Think about it
this way, we're chilling at home in a
good mood. We turn on the
television and hear and feel the

energy of violence and conflict. That triggers anxiety. We may not have thought about it but when we give our attention to the news (which is a low vibrational frequency) it impacts our vibration.

Every sale on television and in most stores, as well as the ads that pop up on our computers, is to get our attention. We are in charge of the purchases for our homes, which means we have influence on how and where we spend our money. The marketers know how valuable we are since we hold the purse strings in the household. Their number one goal is our attention. They know that once they hook us i.e. get our attention, they'll get our money. They tell us how we should dress and what everyone else is wearing. They promise that if we wear what the K family is wearing, our value will be the same. We run out and purchase this have-to-have item thinking it will position us. But all we did was increase the "K" family's millions and possibly put ourselves in debt to "fit in."

In the book, *Ask and It Is Given* by Esther and Jerry Hicks, one of the chapters is titled, "Your Attention Must Be on It, Not the Lack of It."

Another chapter title is, "Giving Your Attention To It Invites It In." Think about where you place your attention – news, celebrity sightings, family drama or money worries. Is that really where you want your attention?

Imagine attention as a lighthouse or a spotlight that shines its ray wherever we point it. Like this spotlight, our attention, when single-focused, is penetrating, responsive, connecting and engaging. Too often

267

we focus our attention on a story
that no longer serves us. We also
focus on past mistakes and perceived
judgments. We rob the present of
possibility at having a different or
more aligned outcome because we're
focused on where we used to be
rather than where we want to go.

Think of this like any other
relationship. What we desire most
from our lover or spouse is their
attention. Our children want our
attention. When our girlfriend calls
upset and crying, she wants our
attention. What does our mother
want? Time and attention. How
about taking that powerful attention
of ours and laser focus it on what *we*
want in *our* life?

I had to redirect myself in this
practice recently. What helped and
propelled me forward was something
I read.

"Stop being afraid of what could go wrong and start being excited about what could go right."

In that moment, I realized I was speaking of a situation I was facing as it was in its current state. I needed to speak of that situation as what I wanted it to evolve into. When we understand the power of our attention, we cultivate the ability to be precise about what we give our attention to. The statement I read moved me to ask myself what I really wanted and look at ways to cultivate that. It didn't ask me to consider whether it would happen or to give any other mental analysis about it. I was to BE present in the moment focused on what I desired. It was so freeing and liberating. My energy immediately shifted to a lighter vibration that felt like hope, possibility and ease. I found myself smiling and excited.

I focused on what could go well and
what could bring relief, rather than
what was right or wrong. Shifting
my attention to what could go well
ultimately shifted my vibration.

PRACTICE

Pay attention to how in charge you
are of your attention throughout the
day. It's important to know what
you're giving your attention to and if
it aligns with your goals.

Pick a day and specific time. During
this period, practice being aware of
where you're focusing your
attention. Ask yourself, "What is my
attention focused on right now?"

Write down what most of your
attention was focused on, how
present you were or if you were on
autopilot with repetitive, internal
mind chatter.

Twin Powers: Intuition & Intention

You have two Superpowers: intuition and intention. I consider these two powers the dynamic duo of energy that show up in different expressions.

Intuition

Intuition wasn't the name by mother gave it. She would simply tell me, "You always know." This was after she had been in a car accident up the street from our house. She was sitting in a parked car with a date, waiting for their take-out food. I magically appeared at the precise moment the car accident took place.

How did I know? The answer was just the beginning of my journey with intuition. I cultivated this relationship over years. From those early years to now I developed a

271

personal relationship with intuition
that is laser focused. I rely on it in all
things, for guidance, inspiration,
confirmation and laughter. I have
grown to ask for guidance on what to
wear, when to make a phone call and
what to speak about.

Many of you have heard of intuition
being referred to as our "sixth sense."
A great movie, starring actor Bruce
Willis, was released with the same
title. We've all heard the still small
voice whisper to our spirit or heart
inner wisdom that resonates at a
deep penetrating level. The level of
clarity it provides us with can be
frightening. The Merriam-Webster
dictionary defines intuition as "the
ability to understand something
immediately without the need for
conscious reasoning." I think that
describes intuition pretty well.

Like my Mom saying, "You always know," intuition is a knowing. Without a doubt, I had that knowing when I ran out of the house as a young girl, yelling as I ran down the street. The power of intuition is in trusting the information being imparted. Some of the ways I've heard intuition described is a hunch, a sense and an inkling. Following are statements used to describe how intuition is experienced:

- I should have followed my first mind.

- Something told me...

- Everything just fell into place.

- I just knew.

Steve Jobs, former CEO of Apple, called intuition more powerful than intellect.

Whether it's our gut feeling or
something that propels us to act,
what we're utilizing is our intuitive
powers. What matters is that we
develop the discipline, willingness
and trust to cultivate this
relationship.

We can get direct information,
wisdom and guidance for our
journey–straight from our Creator. It
doesn't get any better than that. It
doesn't matter whether we think
we're worthy, if we're getting
nudges, hunches or quiet whispers,
then clearly, we are. Some of us
think we don't have the gift of
intuition but most of us do.

Sometimes, we're afraid of what we
hear, or we act like we don't hear it,
but we do.

In a Huffington Post news story,
Sophy Burnham, best-selling author

of the book *The Art of Intuition* wrote,
"It's [intuition] different from
thinking. It's different from logic or
analysis. It is a knowing without
knowing."

Intuition is a feeling. It's words,
fragrances and sounds. Often, it's
persistent and insists on making
itself known, heard and felt. How
many nights have we been awakened
or nudged by our intuition?

Trust me, I've been there. I
remember being awakened in the
middle of the night by persistent
whispers to live my life authentically
and to take the necessary actions to
do just that.

Talk about scary and uncomfortable.
Night after night, I had those
whispers. The more I struggled with
my reality the more fearful I was. I
felt paralyzed to take action until

finally I did. The key to trusting intuition's message was accepting its divine partnership. Commit to listen, trust and follow the wisdom you receive.

PRACTICE

Pick a day and call it your Intuition Day. This will be the day you commit to follow your intuitive guidance. As you go through the day, be alert to what you hear, feel and experience. Become familiar with how intuition feels within you. Grab a journal and make notes about the experience. Document what you felt, how you felt and where you felt it.

Intention

The second superpower is intention. Think of setting an intention like planting seeds in the soil of our subconscious. According to the Merriam-Webster dictionary, intention is "a determination to act in a certain way; or what one intends to do or bring about."

Mega speaker and alternative medicine expert, Deepak Chopra writes "**Intention** is a directed impulse of consciousness that contains the seed form of that which you aim to create."

Through intention we can direct our attention towards a specific plan or purpose. Intention is the starting point of every dream and the fulfillment of our desires. We've heard people speak of setting intentions when starting their day or

setting an intention for a specific
goal.

Intention is a statement about an
outcome we desire to experience.
This is why intention has the power
to influence our experiences.

Intention provides the framework to
set our priorities. Once we set an
intention, we can align with the
resources and opportunities to
manifest it in our life. Setting an
intention activates our heart's desire.
It is a way of communicating to the
Universe that we mean business.
When we set our intention, let it be
compelling. Our thoughts, actions
and resources also need to be in
harmony with the intention.

The more we nurture our seeds with
positive thoughts, feelings and
words, the more we live in alignment
with our desires. Intention is the

creative impulse sent forth into the
Universe that embodies our thoughts
and wishes.

PRACTICE

Give this practice its own time and
space to cultivate the relationship
and become accustomed to the
process. Plan two weeks to a month
to work on this and other practices
individually.

Start the first week of cultivating
your intention practice by spending
time getting clear about the desire
you will be intentional with. Once
you're clear, bring that intention into
the meditation time.

Feel the energy of your intention
fulfilled. This will anchor the
intention within. Let this practice
flow and be light. You're not holding
this tightly. Rather you're

279

communicating with the Universe
with your being, energy and
vibration.

Allow gratitude to seal this session
and let the intention go. When your
15-minute meditation is over, write
the intention five times. Let this
become your ritual. Get in the habit
of setting an intention each morning
during your meditation time. In the
stillness, anchor your intention and
then release your desires. Detach
yourself from the outcome and focus
on living in alignment.

The Strength of Gratitude

In my work as a spiritual minister
and teacher, I've spoken to my and
other congregations. *Unity Spiritual
Center* in Burbank, California invited
me to do monthly sessions. It was
the Thanksgiving holiday. As I
prepared to present, I meditated for

inner wisdom on the theme for that month. At first, I didn't hear or feel anything new.

I was searching for something that would bring peace, understanding and clarity to shift their previously held beliefs. In spite of Thanksgiving being one of the highly marketed holidays, for some it can be challenging to hold onto and express heartfelt gratitude. Whatever we're going through--that car accident, a bout with breast cancer, the death of a loved one--this can prevent us from living in gratitude.

How do we get to gratitude no matter what we experience in our day-to-day living? I made it simple. This method can work for you as well.

I take a deep, slow inhale through my nose. As I exhale, I acknowledge that with each breath I am connected to the divine. I acknowledge that there is a "Presence and a Power," that is breathing my breath and beating my heart.

No matter what I did or didn't do last night. No matter if I lied, laughed, loved, cried or thought I had failed in some way, I trust the Divine Presence giving me life. For in every moment, I am guided back to center–to gratitude.

There is so much written and spoken about gratitude that we can easily become desensitized to expressing heartfelt gratitude. Beyond the unexpected income tax return or the returned favor of a friend, think about how often do we fall asleep expressing gratitude? Are we thankful even for the little things? Things like the sheets, pillows, blankets, the beauty of the landscape that showers us with color in spring.

The abundance of air, rainbows, and breathtaking sunsets.

For many people life is moving at a break-neck pace. Rather than managing our life, we may feel like life is managing us. And for that very reason, gratitude must become our authentic "go-to" practice. Not only are we participating in the divine circulation of life–what we put out comes back–especially if we are intentionally aligning our vibration to receive.

If we pause for a moment and think about how or when we were introduced to the practice of gratitude, it was probably when we were a child. Over the course of our life, how have we shifted our thoughts about giving thanks?

When I was about seven years old, I remember being told to say thank you when someone gave or did something for me. As I got older, I recognized saying thank you is only one side of the coin of gratitude. Gratitude is defined as "a verbal expression for something given or shared."

This works if we want to give thanks. But the other side of gratitude that I want people to explore is the experience of it. I'm not just referring to the perfunctory act of talking or reading about gratitude but living gratitude as a moment-by-moment experience. It is only in this manner we can truly experience the power of gratitude to transform our heart and spirit.

The secret ingredient or power of gratitude is in the way this feeling and energy is activated from within. The feeling of gratitude allows us to access strength in the midst of challenges and disappointments. It is the fertilizer of our soil. With each heartfelt expression, a high energy, high vibrational frequency is activated. When we are willing to accept this process, we come to understand first-hand why the power of gratitude is significant.

Gratitude is significant in our relationship with money because when we're ungrateful, we literally block joy, abundance, money and opportunities. When we're angry with money, it doesn't impact the money per se, it impacts the vibrational frequency that keeps us in alignment with money.

To experience gratitude, take a moment and think of the last time someone did something you were thankful for. They might have shown up when we weren't well. They might have given us a ride when we were stuck and felt overwhelmed. Perhaps they called at just the right moment to talk us off the ledge. Whatever it was, while reflecting on the memory, place your hands over your heart. Now drop the story and feel the feeling that comes up as a result of that experience. That is the power of gratitude. That's what gratitude feels like in our soul.

Gratitude has the power to align our energy with our goals and dreams. This is the *experience* of gratitude rather than the idea of it.

Once we make time to bask in the energy of gratitude, we can take the next step. Be bold enough to be in gratitude for what we've asked for *before* it shows up. Yep, you read that right. In the quiet time, practice being grateful for what is to come. Be thankful for what you've already meditated on, visioned about or

released an affirmative prayer for.
Just feel grateful knowing that it or
something better, is on the way.

PRACTICE

Pick a time each day to pause and
bask in the feeling of gratitude. It
may be at lunch time. Walk outside
and look at the sky, trees, clouds and
flowers. Inhale and give thanks for
breath.

Exhale and give thanks for the
process that happens without any
assistance from you. Feel the feeling
of it and then return to whatever is to
be done next.

Journal about how you feel in that
moment and even for the rest of the
day. Taking part in this practice can
position us for alignment. Get in the
habit of feeling gratitude each day–
the shower is a great place for

spontaneous joy. Also get in the
habit of creating a running list of
things you're grateful for.

Create your Gratitude Journal.
Commit your desires and dreams by
making daily entries of gratitude for
perfect divine timing in all your
affairs.
This practice will replace your
tendency to complain, while
elevating your capacity to receive.
There are two sides to giving
gratitude. On one hand, we give and
on the other, we must be open to
receive. The two go hand-in-hand.

The Bliss of Appreciation

Finally, the most expansive and
joyful practice that will skyrocket us
into a higher energy is a form of
appreciation called, "raving." I
learned about raving from the *Divine
Openings* book by Lola Jones. What

caught my attention was the level of enthusiasm this practice ignites within. It literally kicks your gratitude up a notch. Let me tell you what raving is about.

I embraced the practice after attending several five-day silent retreats in Texas. After attending the first retreat, I made raving a practice to begin my mornings and end my evenings. I'd take five or ten minutes while in bed to rave about what I appreciated. My focus was on how positive or amazing something could be or was in my life. This became my way to train my mind and shift my mindset.

Raving is about joy and excitement. To rave is nothing more than sharing pure joy, excitement, utter amazement and heartfelt celebration for what is. It is a very passionate and expressive manner in which you celebrate everything. The vibration of raving is equivalent to love. Imagine starting your day in full appreciation of the clarity, fulfillment, joy, opportunities, answers, and stillness you will experience that day.

Picture this...you just got it! Whatever IT is, you just received it! You waited so long to have it! You aligned everything to get it and now here it is! You can barely believe it! It happened!!! You're jumping up and down screaming. Tears are streaming down your face as the realization that all your dreams are coming true. What do you do? You run to the phone to tell someone. But instead of picking up the phone to call someone, you turn inward.

You ecstatically offer appreciation and joy. You are raving!!

I became a huge fan of raving to such a degree that for years I kept a raving journal. Then I took the raving practice with me and would rave wherever I was. I continue to blast into raving as I witness events and actions that seem to fall into place.

I rave about whatever triggers my flow of emotions. I rave about things like a multi-colored rose. I mean, how does that happen since the seed was only one color? I rave about a tree trunk pushing up through the soil spreading like a bench to sit on. The brilliant color of a lavender bougainvillea plant on the trellis of every corner in southern California. I rave about the downpour of rain, the majestic full moon, the journey of a leaf falling to the ground. There is so much we can rave about.

Just recently I was awakened by the song of an owl in the early morning.

Now that was something to rave about.

I have found that raving has a profound impact on elevating our energy and experiences. When we are wrapped in the embrace of raving, we automatically align with the energy that brings forth the greatest results.

When we turn to the Universe, when we follow its guidance, things turn out just as we envisioned and planned. Rave when that thing was perfectly orchestrated. Rave when the mountain was moved out of your way. Rave when a prayer was answered. Rave because the surgery happened with grace and ease.

Here's the thing, we're not necessarily raving to our friends or family, even though that would be nice.

Our first instinct is to run and tell someone what happened. Instead, take the joy and heart-felt appreciation and giving it to the Universe, Source and the Divine. Returning to the Source allows us to participate in a divine dance of love.

Feeling and expressing appreciation takes our energy to a high vibration beyond expressing thanks. Remember the energy of appreciation is the energy of love. Love is the highest vibration we can access. Appreciation is embracing love, delight, surprise and astonishment. It is a one-on-one internal experience between you and the Universe.

Practice-*Morning & Evening Raves*

Upon awakening and going to bed
express verbally or internally, your
appreciation for everything.

At the same time, train your mind to
look for what's good. Look for things
your heart can express daily
appreciation for. It's all around you if
you look for it.

Conclusion

Now! is the most powerful word to bring the results we desire and deserve. We've come a long way. We can continue to make progress toward achieving our dreams. Position yourself for alignment, action and results.

This process is what I guide my clients through at the beginning of us working together. They gain clarity and design a blueprint to follow. This step-by-step process is effective in beginning our creative process.

First things first. Let's identify what you want to manifest. Think of Steven Covey who offered us the principle of starting with the end in mind. Where do we want to end up?

Take out the journal and fill in the blanks.

"I desire to manifest _____.

To help those I coach get laser clarity, I suggest this practice.

1. What do you want?

Example: I want a nice vacation.

2. What do you NOT want?

Example: I don't want to worry about bills.

Now that we're clear about what you want and don't want, what's the flip side of each thing you listed?

Example:

I desire to feel more confident about how I handle my money.

I desire to make choices with my money that will build my savings.

I desire to face my credit card debt.

Make sense?

Then to empower your words, add the feeling you desire as the result of achieving this goal.

Example: I desire to manifest an additional month of money in my checking account so that I will feel _____ (you fill in the blank).

Or I will feel _____ (fill in the blank) when I live each day knowing I have money in my checking account.

Next, begin to **imagine**. Ask yourself
what it will feel like when your desire
becomes a reality.

What will it feel like to have money
in a savings account?

How amazing will it be for you to
build wealth through investing?

How strong will you feel as you learn
to build wealth through real estate or
investments?

Think of this as your daydream
energy. Your writing will say:

I feel...

I am raving about...

I feel safe.

I feel calm, confident and peaceful.

Lastly, **align** with what you desire to see manifest in your life. You will accomplish this by deciding what it will feel like to HAVE what you desire.

Take time to capture the feeling of what you imagined. How will your life be different? What will feel different for you by having what you desire? Explore this like a daydream— light and easy.

Remember it was Einstein who told us that "imagination is more important than knowledge." Take the time to *imagine* your life the way you desire and deserve.

Imagine one paycheck or one client payment for your coaching program sitting in your bank account and growing your savings. Imagine taking a vacation and money NOT being an issue.

Imagine your bills being on autopay. Imagine how you feel inside. Einstein also said, "Knowledge is limited, whereas imagination embraces the entire world, stimulating progress, giving birth to evolution." Imagine it!

The next action to take is to join me for the Money Mastery Now – Align with Money workshop. This 3-system process is designed to help you unlock your prosperity and become a vibrational match for your results. Detailed information is in the Resources Section.

Repeat after me:

"Now (fill in your name) is the time for you to create more, increase your wealth, live a prosperous life and find happiness in everyday relationships."

You can upgrade your relationship with money from strained to a friendship or partnership by recognizing that you are made of the same energy that your dreams, desires and goals are made of.

Affirmations are great. To support you on your personal journey of money mastery, there's a link in the Resources section for a complimentary gift. Your *Money Mastery Now* affirmation cards. These cards will position you to be intentional with your thoughts, words, feelings and actions. You want to believe in the affirmations you release into the universe. Make sure you speak them out loud and during meditation. Especially the ones that resonate with your spirit and heart. Make an emotional connection which will activate the energy of the affirmation.

I suggest writing out affirmations at least 25 times a week. You must make an internal shift in order for affirmations to produce the external results you're looking for.

I look forward to meeting you at one of my Masterclasses or in the Money Mastery Now! Intensive.

Resources

PRINT RESOURCES:

The Emotional Life of Money: How Money Changes the Way We Think and Feel by Mary Cross

Real Money Answers For Every Woman, by Patrice C. Washington How To Win The Money Game With or Without A Man

Think and Grow Rich, by Napoleon Hill

Abundance Now: Amplify Your Life & Achieve Prosperity Today, by Lisa Nichols

Things Are Going Great In My Absence: How to Let Go & Let God Do the Heavy Lifting, by Lola Jones

Let's Get You Happy First 4 Steps To Get You To Your Happy, Jenenne R. Macklin

The One Week Budget. Learn to Create Your Money Management System in 7 Days or Less, by The Budgetnista

Women & Money: Owning the Power to Control Your Destiny, by Suze Orman

75 Avoidable Mistakes Women Make With Money, by Lois P. Frankel, PhD

The Law of Attraction and *The Teachings of Abraham,* by Esther & Jerry Hicks

Warrior Goddess Training: Become the Woman You Are Meant to Be, by Heatherash Amara

The Prosperity Factor: How to Achieve Unlimited Wealth in Every Area of Your Life, by Joe Vitale

Spiritual Economics: The Principles and Process of True Prosperity, by Eric Butterworth

Sacred Woman: A Guide to Healing the Feminine Body, Mind and Spirit, by Queen Afua

Radical Forgiveness, by Colin Tipping

A Revolutionary Five-Stage Process to Heal Relationship

ONLINE RESOURCES:

Radical Forgiveness
www.radicalforgiveness.com/freetools

MONEY MASTERY NOW!

Affirmation Cards

[www.jenennemacklin.com/affirmati ons](www.jenennemacklin.com/affirmations)

Ready to act? Start here with your personal affirmation cards. Use these affirmation cards to speak, think, feel and take-action in alignment with goals and desired results.

This deck is created to offer you intentional affirmations for your thoughts and words. Honor your feelings and taking inspired action.

307

Money Mastery Now Prosperity Quiz

www.jenennemacklin.com/Prosperity

Ready to identify how close you are to your goal of living in prosperity?

Ready to know what action you can take to live in greater prosperity?

The Prosperity Quiz reveals the hidden habits, unconscious behaviors and thoughts that sabotage your connection with prosperity.

After you take your quiz be sure to schedule your Money Mastery Now Strategy Session.

Money Mastery Now: My Relationship with Money Quiz

www.jenennemacklin.com/moneyquiz

How do you feel about budgeting, for real?

What are your basic needs versus your wants?

How much do your feelings, inherited beliefs and historical stories impact your relationships?

This quiz focuses on exposing your daily actions in your relationship with money.

Align with Money Now

www.jenennemacklin.com/align

This powerful, mindset shifting, 3-Step System is designed to help those who are tired of having a dysfunctional relationship with money.

The 3-Step System is also for those who are: Tired of secretly struggling with money while falling deeper and deeper into a pit.

Ready to stop chasing money and get out of the debt loop–once and for all.

Ready to increase your money flow, live a fulfilling life and find happiness in your everyday relationships.

Understand your value and start charging for your value in your business.

Stop feeling stupid and gain money confidence to handle your finances and achieve your goals.

Money Mastery Now Strategy Session

Believe it or not, your thoughts, feelings and fears around money affect your "goal getting" abilities in life and business.

When you're ready to conquer your fears around success, wealth and financial prosperity...let's connect. Schedule your complimentary Money Mastery Nowsession here:

Time trade Link:
https://my.timetrade.com/book/2R
R6C

Appreciation

To my guardian angels, my teachers, guides, and ancestors who continue to walk with me though unseen. Your Presence is deeply felt. I appreciate and acknowledge your early morning nudges, insights, powerful wisdom and gentle whispers of guidance and encouragement. Your eternal love surrounds me. Your wisdom guides me. Your strength and power continue to sustain me. I stand on your shoulders.

To my first coach Lisa Nichols:
I express heartfelt appreciation for your gift, coaching insights, and for creating the powerful transformative space of Speak and Write to Make Millions and so much more.

This project was birthed in the transformational space of Speak and

Write. In spite of having the idea written down, including chapters and titles, the book remained an idea on paper that I pushed around my desk. In 2018 I followed my own coaching advice of, "complete what you start," and committed to bring forth the teachings from my experience and journey to empower others.

To the amazing women of the Real Money Matters group: I express heartfelt appreciation for your time, wisdom, insights and transparency. Thank you for helping me gain a greater understanding of what we do and why we do what we do – with our money.

To Tonya Brewington, Ifalade TaShia Asanti and Geevani Singh I express nothing but gratitude and appreciation for your time input, skills and belief in this project. You have been patience, and diligent, to labor over my writings and edit them to bring it into some cohesive presentation I extend a heartfelt, "Thank you."!

ACKNOWLEDGEMENTS

About the Author

Visionary catalyst and sought-after speaker, Jenenne Macklin is on a mission to empower one million women to create their most fulfilling, successful and prosperous lives by 2023, and to eradicate, "Scarcity Thinking," on the planet.

A widely respected spiritual teacher, and an influential wealth mentor and author, Jenenne stands in her knowing that we all have been given everything we need to create and live the life we desire. Drawing on her laser-sharp intuition, 25+ years of personal and professional experiences, Jenenne empowers women with proven principles and tangible practices to boldly create wealthy lives and businesses. With clients ranging from celebrities and millionaire entrepreneurs, to conscious women and small business

317

owners, Jenenne inspires significant internal shifts that produce real, visible results in life or business.

Abandoned at birth and placed in an orphanage, Jenenne was later adopted by two loving parents, one of which was her biological father (that's a story for her next book). She made peace with this scenario by recognizing that she had been blessed by two women: one who gave her life and another who gave her love. It was these humble beginnings that sparked the flame that fueled her passion for truth and love. It also gave her permission to freely embrace forgiveness and stand in her new-found personal power! This became the source of her commitment to empower women to release hurt, fear, and doubt in order to embrace true financial freedom. Jenenne allowed what was once a painful experience to shift her consciousness. Jenenne looks forward to empowering you to do the same!

Jenenne was born in Omaha, Nebraska, and now resides in Pasadena, California.

ACKNOWLEDGEMENTS